1955   £8   HC
                RIS

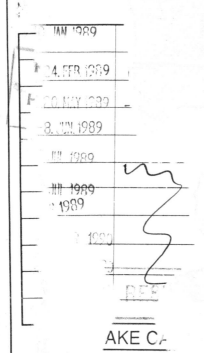
343-1

UNITED IN CRIME

H. MONTGOMERY HYDE

UNITED IN CRIME

"Divisés d'interêts et par les crimes unis."
Voltaire

WILLIAM HEINEMANN LTD
MELBOURNE :: LONDON :: TORONTO

FIRST PUBLISHED 1955

PRINTED IN GREAT BRITAIN
AT THE WINDMILL PRESS
KINGSWOOD, SURREY

To
BOODLE

CONTENTS

ILLUSTRATIONS

ACKNOWLEDGMENTS

Substantial parts of this book have previously appeared in print, namely in the London *Evening Standard*, *Everybody's*, the Manchester *Evening Chronicle*, and the provincial newspapers which take the feature service supplied by the Central Press, Ltd. I am grateful to the editors of these journals for kindly enabling me to republish them in this form.

I am also indebted to the editor of the *News of the World* for permission to quote an account of a case recently described in its pages.

The following illustrations are reproduced from the Notable British Trials Series by permission of the publishers, William Hodge & Co., Ltd.—I.R.A. bomb outrage at Coventry (from the *Trial of Peter Barnes and Others*); the yard with the drums used by Haigh (from the *Trial of John George Haigh*); Edith Thompson and Frederick Bywaters (from the *Trial of Bywaters and Thompson*); and George Chapman (from the *Trial of George Chapman*).

The remaining illustrations are reproduced by courtesy of *Picture Post*, *Picture Press*, *Topical Press* and William Heinemann Ltd.   H. M. H.

FOREWORD ON CRIME

HOWEVER we may try to account for it, the distressing fact remains that the prevalence of crime in this country has increased greatly, compared with what it was before the last war. In 1938 the number of indictable offences known to the police in England and Wales was 283,220. In 1951 the number was 524,506, nearly double the pre-war figure. It is true that at the time of writing (1954) there are some welcome signs of a general decrease in crime—the figures for 1952 were 513,559 and for 1953 they were 472,989—but today the volume of crime is still far above what it was in the immediate pre-war years. Even in the past two years, in spite of the general drop, there has been an increase in particular types of crime, notably violence against the person and sexual offences.*

There is one kind of sexual offender who has increased in numbers during the period under review. This is the male homosexual. One judge of assize recently described it as "perfectly appalling that when judges went out on circuit they found the criminal calendars packed full of cases of indecent assault and gross indecency between males". In 1938 there were 134 cases of sodomy and bestiality known to the police in England and Wales. The number in 1952 was 670. The number of attempts to commit unnatural offences, including indecent assaults, increased during the same period from 822 to 3,087. Offences of gross indecency between male persons increased from 320 to 1,686. In giving these figures to the House of Commons the Under-Secretary for Home Affairs (Sir Hugh Lucas-Tooth) stated that he had no corresponding figures for importuning by male persons, but in 1952 proceedings were taken in 373 cases in the Metropolitan police district, 'a very large number'. Over this period indictable offences of this kind have increased between fourfold and fivefold. "I

* See Home Office. *Criminal Statistics England and Wales* 1953; also statement by Home Secretary in House of Commons, April 14, 1954.

cannot give the House any opinion for the reasons for that increase," the Minister went on, "and I think I can say with complete truth that the reasons are simply not known. Quite clearly, this is a problem which calls for very careful consideration on the part of those responsible for the welfare of the nation."

Popular conscience has recently been stirred by the prosecution of three public figures for this type of offence, the defendants respectively being a Labour Member of Parliament, a peer of the realm and a well-known actor. The cases of Mr. W. J. Field, formerly M.P. for South Paddington, Lord Montagu of Beaulieu and Sir John Gielgud have left no doubt in the public mind that homosexuality is not confined to people in relatively humble positions in this country. These cases served to stimulate a general demand that some kind of authoritative action should be taken. This began with an outspoken leading article on the subject in the *Sunday Times* (November 1, 1953), which in turn elicited a large number of letters addressed to the editor in that journal's correspondence columns. Shortly afterwards a group of Anglican clergy and doctors, working under the auspices of the Church of England Moral Welfare Council, published an interesting and valuable report, in which the strongest arguments were put forward for an official inquiry.* This was followed by a debate in the House of Commons in which representatives from both sides of the House combined to ask the Home Secretary to appoint a Royal Commission to investigate the law relating to and the medical treatment of homosexuality. In the result the Home Secretary, along with the Secretary of State for Scotland, agreed to the appointment of a Committee, which he felt to be more appropriate than a Royal Commission, to examine this question and the 'parallel' problem of the law relating to prostitution and solicitation generally.†

The existence of a variety of legal anomalies is as unjust as it is irrational. It is only male homosexuality which is penalised

---

* *The Problem of Homosexuality. An Interim Report.* The Church Magazine, November, 1953.

† Parliamentary Debates. Commons, April 28, 1954. Cols. 1745–1750.

by our law. There is nothing in English law which regards homosexual practices between females as criminal and no serious attempt has been made by Parliament to make them so. Yet such practices on the part of 'Lesbian' women are by no means unknown in this country. Furthermore, under the Criminal Law Amendment Act 1885, Section 11, acts of indecency between males are indictable offences, *even if committed in private*. As the Report of the Church of England Moral Welfare Council points out, in no other department of life does the State hold itself competent to interfere with private actions of consenting adults which are not demonstrably anti-social. (These must not be confused with certain adult actions which are quite clearly anti-social, such as incest, both from the biological and the domestic standpoint). On the other hand, a man may commit the commonly regarded moral sin of fornication without making himself liable to any criminal proceeding, although grave social consequences may follow for the illegitimate offspring who may result from his action. Another legal anomaly is seen in the differing penalties attached to male and female importuning. While a woman prostitute is liable to a maximum penalty of £2 for 'soliciting', her male counterpart may on conviction be sent to prison for two years as a 'rogue and vagabond'.

Of course, the young of both sexes must be protected from seduction and assault, and it is the duty of the State to afford them this protection, as well as to preserve public decency. No sane individual would suggest that the perversion of a boy or youth by an older man should not be punishable, whether or not the act complained of was committed with the consent of the younger person. Unfortunately the law, as it stands today, actually defeats its purpose. It is indisputable that the Act of 1885 greatly increased the loathsome trade of the blackmailer. Indeed, shortly after it was passed, one judge described it as 'the blackmailer's charter' and there is no doubt that money has been extorted in countless cases during the past seventy years under threat of denunciation to the police. This has encouraged older male homosexuals to seduce inexperienced boys as less likely to think of blackmail and easier to cajole or browbeat into a pledge of secrecy. In this respect at least it is arguable that the continuance of the present law is actually the indirect cause of harm to children and young people.

It is probably true to say that no case of homosexuality, since that of Oscar Wilde and his co-defendant Alfred Taylor in 1895, has attracted such notoriety as the trial of Lord Montagu and his associates, Michael Pitt-Rivers and Peter Wildeblood, at Winchester Assizes in the spring of 1954. Both cases, like many others involving lesser folk, had two particular features in common, which cannot escape consideration and indeed severe criticism in any investigation of the law relating to this type of offence. The principal defendants in each case were convicted on the evidence of self-confessed accomplices, who were granted immunity by the Crown as a reward for 'turning Queen's Evidence'. They were also individually charged, not only with committing specific acts of indecency, but also with 'conspiring with others to commit them'.

The fact that the offence is committed in private means that in practically every case the only way in which the Crown can obtain evidence sufficient to warrant a prosecution is through the means of an accomplice. Now an accomplice's evidence is always tainted and it requires corroboration. In both the Wilde and Montagu cases corroboration was forthcoming in the shape of the admitted entertainment by the accused of the accomplices who were in a different social class from the accused and also in the writing by the accused of letters containing expressions of endearment. But why should the accomplices get off scot-free while their partners in crime, who are equally guilty under the present law, should be punished, often with exemplary severity? Accomplices in this type of offence are almost invariably actuated by such ignoble motives as jealousy, fear and blackmail, when they agree to go into the witness-box and testify against the wretched man in the dock. In the opinion of many it is a standing reproach to our legal system that convictions for homosexual offences should be obtained in this way, and most intelligent people today will agree that it is extremely doubtful whether the cause of justice is served in the long run by such methods.

Similar considerations apply to the issue of conspiracy, particularly in such cases as these, where the addition to the indictment of a conspiracy charge makes the words and acts of each of the defendants admissible in evidence against all the others. The effect of this device has recently been well expressed by a distinguished American judge. "A co-defendant in a conspiracy trial occupies an uneasy seat," said Justice Jackson in the United States Supreme Court in 1949. "There generally will be evidence of wrong-doing by somebody. It is difficult for the individual to make his own case stand on its merits in the minds of jurors who are ready to believe that birds of a feather are flocked together. If he is silent he is taken to admit it; and if, as often happens, co-defendants can be prodded into accusing or contradicting each other, they convict each other." In our own country the use of the conspiracy charge has been severely condemned by the Court of Criminal Appeal, and in the case of prosecutions under the Act of 1885, at least, there is much to be said for revising this branch of the law.

The administration of the law has another objectionable feature. It has been alleged—certainly it has never been officially denied—that police are used as *agents provocateurs* to ensnare homosexuals into incriminating themselves by word or gesture. It seems that plain-clothes policemen frequent public lavatories in the metropolis for this purpose and that among those who have walked into this trap was the unfortunate Mr. Field. It is an unsavoury kind of police action and many people have an uneasy conscience about it. There is always the danger too that it may open the door to police corruption, since it provides the unscrupulous police officer with an easy opportunity for 'framing' the author of an innocent smile or harmless remark. There is also the chance of the police being genuinely mistaken, as appears from the following account recently published in the *News of the World* (June 6, 1954):

"An appalling mistake has been made by the police," said Mr. Ellison Rich at the Guildhall, London, when he defended the Rev. Frank Herbert F——, aged 51, Vicar of L——.
The case against F——, who was charged with im-

portuning at Liverpool Street station, was dismissed.

Mr. C. J. Thackery, prosecuting, said that on the night of Sunday, May 9, two police officers watched F—— in a lavatory at the station from 11.15 to 11.45. When arrested F—— vehemently denied he had done anything improper and insisted on a medical examination. The doctor's report supported F——'s statement up to a point.

"But," added Mr. Thackery, "I am not calling the doctor because my case rests on the police evidence."

F——, in evidence, denied the charge. He had given an explanation, which a doctor found to be correct. This was consistent with his innocence.

He changed his clothes before coming to the City because he found it a relaxation to drop the clerical collar after a hard day's work.

The Bishop of B—— and other witnesses testified to F——'s high moral character. The Bishop said he always picked out a particularly good man for the living of L——. He had every confidence in F——.

Mr. Rich said he did not suggest that the charge had been concocted by the police, but he did suggest that a most appalling mistake had been made.

Since the object of the exercise is to catch adult homosexuals in search of similarly minded adults, an alteration in the law would have the effect, among others, of releasing the police from the performance of an extremely unpleasant duty.

To the great majority of British people the idea of male homosexual intercourse is as morally repugnant and sinful as adultery, if not more so. But few of us today, even north of the Border, would wish to see adultery restored to the category of criminal offences, although like homosexuality it was once punishable by death under our penal code. Homosexual conduct between women and the practice of sexual perversions between female prostitutes and their male clients are also ethically reprehensible, but such acts are not punishable under our law. Of course, homosexuality between consenting adults of both sexes, adultery and prostitution, must be distinguished from other acts like public indecency, importuning and, above all, corruption of the young, against which the public is entitled to be protected and which must continue to be treated as legal crimes. But the case for the reform of the law as regards homosexual adult males is long overdue and in conformity with what has already taken place in most other European countries.

There is another form of crime which merits particular consideration, partly by reason of its nature and underlying motives and partly because in peace-time it is the only offence for which in practice the death sentence is imposed in the United Kingdom. It is the crime of murder. For the reasons I have given, it excites public interest more than any other in the judicial calendar. Furthermore, it is the only offence for which at present the court has no discretion to determine the appropriate sentence.

For the past fifty years three people on the average have been murdered every week in Britain. During the first half of the present century (1900–1949) there were approximately 7,500 cases of murder in England and Wales and 600 in Scotland known to the police. 1,080 men and 130 women were convicted of this crime and sentenced to death in England and Wales, and 54 men and 5 women in Scotland. The number of those executed in England and Wales was 632 (621 men and 11 women) and in Scotland 23 (22 men and 1 woman). In the years of peace the number of murders known to the police has tended to remain fairly stable in proportion to the population, but the figures have naturally tended to rise in war and immediate postwar years. However, the annual average over the fifty years is approximately the same as for the first decade of the century, namely 149 in England and Wales (3.89 per million of the population) and 12 in Scotland (2.52 per million of the population).

As the recent Report of the Royal Commission on Capital Punishment points out, there is perhaps no single class of offences that varies so widely both in character and in culpability as that of murder as defined in our law. The murderers may be men, women, youths, girls or hardly older than children. They may be normal, feeble-minded, neurotic, epileptic or insane. The crime may be understandable and pitiable, or callous and brutal, it may be unpremeditated or carefully planned, or it may be committed in the course of carrying out another crime. There may be no murderous intent and the victim's death may depend on an accident. The underlying motives demonstrate a wide range of human emotions, such as cupidity, revenge, lust, jealousy, anger, fear, pity, despair, duty, self-righteousness and political fanatacism.

Yet for all these varieties of murder our courts have no alternative but to pronounce sentence of death, once the accused has been found guilty by a jury, although the generally accepted view today is that the supreme penàlty should be reserved for the more heinous cases. Our law still demands a life for a life, as it did in primitive times, regardless of the circumstances. Unlike some other countries, such as the United States, where capital punishment is inflicted, there are no degrees of murder in the United Kingdom. But in practice the inflexibility of the law is mitigated by the exercise of the royal prerogative of mercy, through the Home Secretary in England and Wales and the Secretary of State for Scotland north of the River Tweed. Out of approximately 1,200 sentenced to death in England and Wales during the 1900–1949 period, 400, or one in three, were reprieved and had their sentences commuted to life imprisonment. (The figures for Scotland were approximately one in two, i.e. 59 death sentences and 32 reprieves). There is a further mitigating factor in the reluctance of juries to see the death sentence imposed in particular cases, which sometimes leads them to return verdicts not in accordance with the facts. Giving evidence before the recent Royal Commission on Capital Punishment, Lord Justice Denning, a most experienced trial judge, declared that "in many cases which are in law plain murder, juries return verdicts of manslaughter, because they do not think the death sentence is appropriate". It is significant that the Howard League for Penal Reform have stated that their observations over many years bear out Lord Justice Denning's view.

Juries in murder trials also add recommendations to mercy

to verdicts of guilty, sometimes under the impression that the murderer will be automatically reprieved in consequence. But this by no means invariably happens. Between the years 1900 and 1948, 360 men and 108 women were found guilty of murder in England and Wales and recommended to mercy by the jury. Out of these, 108 men (a little less than one in three) and 4 women were eventually hanged. Reprieves were granted to 74 per cent of those recommended to mercy (68 per cent of men and 95 per cent of women).* Even where the judge has concurred in the jury's recommendation to mercy, the Home Secretary has not always found himself able to follow it, although he is very reluctant to disregard a recommendation of this kind in these circumstances. Such cases are comparatively rare. In the period 1900–1949 there were only six cases in England and Wales and one in Scotland where the death sentence was carried out in the face of a recommendation to mercy in which the trial judge had concurred. Another such case occurred in England in 1953, when Derek Bentley, a youth of nineteen, was hanged for his part in the murder of a police officer, despite a recommendation to mercy by the jury in which the Lord Chief Justice, Lord Goddard, who tried the case, appeared to concur. This particular case is of additional interest because the hand which fired the fatal shot was not Bentley's but that of his companion-in-crime Christopher Craig, who was only sixteen. The unfortunate Bentley is apparently the first individual in our legal history to have been hanged as an accomplice in a murder for which the principal in the first degree could not be executed on grounds of age.†

The members of the last Royal Commission on Capital Punishment were precluded by their terms of reference from considering whether the abolition of the supreme penalty for murder would be desirable. They were restricted to the question of the modification or limitation of the present liability

* The corresponding figures for Scotland were 28 men and 3 women recommended to mercy, of whom 8 men and 1 woman were executed. Reprieves were granted to 68 per cent of those recommended to mercy (68 per cent of men and 67 per cent of women).

† See the *Trial of Craig and Bentley*, edited by the present writer (Notable British Trials Series), 1954.

to the death penalty for this particular crime. In their Report they rejected any proposal for degrees of murder so as to confine the death penalty to the more heinous cases. They also rejected the proposal to give the judge power to substitute a lesser sentence, but they looked with favour upon the alternative of allowing the jury to decide in each case whether life imprisonment can properly be substituted for the death penalty. Their conclusion was that a workable scheme on the latter lines could be devised and that it was "the only practicable way of enabling the courts, instead of the Executive, to take account of extenuating circumstances so as to correct the rigidity which is the outstanding defect of the existing law".*

The only advantage of such a scheme as this would be to relieve the Home Secretary and Secretary of State for Scotland of their present responsibilities in respect of convictions for murder by transferring them to juries. This would involve a fundamental change in the traditional functions of British juries and, as the Royal Commission realised, would not be without practical difficulties. It cannot be regarded as a satisfactory solution. The real issue is whether capital punishment ought to be retained or abolished.

Today the United Kingdom and France are the only major European Powers which continue to inflict the death penalty for murder. The abolitionist States include the Scandinavian and Benelux countries, Italy, Portugal, Switzerland, Western Germany and Austria. In England an amendment to the Criminal Justice Act 1948, providing for the suspension of the death penalty for a trial period of five years, was carried in the House of Commons by a relatively narrow majority (245 to 222) on a free vote: it was subsequently rejected by an overwhelming majority of the Lords (181 to 21) and thus failed to become law. It is significant that abolition of capital punishment for murder has never been followed by any increase in this type of crime, nor has its temporary restoration, e.g., in Italy between 1931 and 1948, been followed by a decrease. Indeed the reverse is apt to be the case. In England, during the period of four weeks between the passing of the Commons

* Report of Royal Commission on Capital Punishment 1949–1953, at p. 278.

amendment abolishing capital punishment and its rejection by the Lords, when the death penalty was suspended, murders averaged three per week. In the immediately following six weeks after the death penalty was restored, the average rose to 4.6 a week. Consequently, in the words of the last Royal Commission's Report, "it is important to view this question in a just perspective and not to base a penal policy in relation to murder on exaggerated estimates of the uniquely deterrent force of the death penalty".

There are five main methods of judicial execution of criminals in use in the Western World today. They are hanging, guillotining, electrocution, gassing and shooting. The first of these has been the method employed in the United Kingdom for many centuries: that the condemned person shall be 'hanged by the neck till dead'. In former times this form of punishment, by publicly displaying the criminal in the most ignominious and abject of postures, besides being in itself a peculiarly slow and painful end since the victim gradually died of suffocation, was calculated to act as a powerful deterrent in the minds of the onlookers by inspiring an exceptional dread. In the nineteenth century some of the more barbarous and repulsive features of hanging were removed. Executions in public were discontinued and the 'long drop' was introduced in an effort to make death instantaneous by dislocating the vertebræ. But, in spite of this latter innovation, the task was sometimes bungled. In 1885 a condemned murderer was reprieved after three unsuccessful attempts had been made to hang him in Exeter Prison. There were other 'untoward occurrences', to use the Royal Commission's euphemistic language. In other words, a man was sometimes given too short a drop and died slowly of strangulation, while on other occasions the drop was too long, with the result that he was decapitated. As the result of a number of scientific recommendations made about the length of drop, improvements in the apparatus of the scaffold, and certain preliminary tests and precautions, we are assured by the Home Office experts that this method of execution, as carried out in Her Majesty's prisons for many years past, is speedy, certain and humane.

Nevertheless, hanging remains a singularly revolting and unpleasant business for all in any way concerned with it. Beginning with the awful moment when the judge dons the black cap in court and pronounces the death sentence, there is the agonising and long-drawn-out experience of the condemned cell, culminating in the ghastly scene in the adjacent execution chamber. To read the Home Office memorandum on the subject of arrangements for an execution, with its complacent remarks about the cell being 'equipped to accommodate the prisoner' with such 'amenities' as cards, chess and dominoes, newspapers and books, and about the Governor calling on him before 'the prisoner retires for the night to talk to him and give him an opportunity of saying anything he may wish', we might imagine, in the words of Lord Templewood in his eloquent book *The Shadow of the Gallows*, that we are dealing with a well-run hotel and an assiduous Swiss manager looking after the comfort of his guests. In fact, behind this superficially attractive picture there are many sinister details.

There is the constant watching of the condemned man night and day by two warders in his cell and at exercise lest he should cheat the gallows of its prey.

> And by each side a Warder walked,
> For fear the man might die.

There is the hangman peering from some hidden vantage point to assess the prisoner's weight; there is the preliminary testing of the execution 'apparatus' with a bag of sand attached to the rope which is to be used for the hanging; there are painful visits from the prisoner's relatives, whom he is only permitted to see from behind a partition; there are the ministrations of the Medical Officer and the exhortations of the Chaplain.

> The Governor was strong upon
> The Regulations Act,
> The Doctor said that Death was but
> A scientific fact,
> And twice a day the Chaplain called,
> And left a little tract.

Above all there is the mounting tension throughout the prison, rising to a terrible crescendo as the final scene is enacted, with the grim procession entering the condemned cell, the reading of the burial service for a living person, his being led to the scaffold and placed across the division of the trap, the pinioning of the prisoner's arms and legs by the executioner, the white cap being placed over his head, the adjustment of the noose, the pulling of the lever. . . .

> And as one sees most fearful things
> In the crystal of a dream,
> We saw the greasy hempen rope
> Hooked to the blackened beam
> And heard the prayer the hangman's snare
> Strangled into a scream.

The execution which Oscar Wilde described in such moving verses in *The Ballad of Reading Gaol* took place at Reading during his imprisonment there in 1896. The condemned man was a trooper in the Royal Horse Guards, named Charles Thomas Wooldridge, who was hanged for the murder of his wife. According to a local account, Wooldridge is said to have cut his wife's throat "in a very determined manner, she having excited his jealousy and (so far as the evidence went) greatly annoyed him". The *Ballad* was dedicated to his memory.

> The man had killed the thing he loved
> And so he had to die.

Today the church bell no longer tolls and the black flag no longer flutters from the prison walls. Nor are the prisoners locked in their cells when an execution is taking place as they were in Wilde's time. But other objectionable features remain. The body of the prisoner is still left hanging for an hour after execution, although we are assured on authority that the prisoner loses consciousness within a few seconds of the drop and life becomes extinct very shortly afterwards. Undesirable publicity continues to be attracted by the posting of the notice of an impending execution on the prison gate as well as the notice that the execution has been carried out.* There is also the effect of the performance of duties connected with an execution on the prison staff and the general atmosphere of strain in the prison which affects the other prisoners. The latest Royal Commission on Capital Punishment tends to minimise these effects in its Report and dismiss them as short-lived. A former Home Secretary, Lord Templewood, takes a different view which I am inclined to think is nearer the mark. "There is no doubt," he writes, "that in spite of much of the official evidence to the contrary, an execution has a most disturbing effect upon the inmates of a prison, whether staff or prisoners".

Ellis, the executioner, tried to take his own life after he had hanged Mrs. Thompson in 1923, and we know from the admission of both the Governor and the Chaplain of Holloway Prison at the time that execution took place how much they personally were affected by the whole affair. Indeed the Chaplain was so shocked that after his retirement he devoted most of his time to speaking and writing in favour of the abolition of the death penalty. Then there was the inquest of a retired chief warder who had committed suicide, where it was stated that he had attended between twenty and thirty executions, as a result of which he "slept very little and worried a lot". He left a letter saying "I cannot face these dreadful nights any longer".

The latest Royal Commission has recommended that we continue to hang our convicted murderers, so long as capital punishment is retained in this country. Its members considered and rejected other methods such as electrocution and the gas-chamber, which they did not feel on balance has any advantage over hanging as now carried out in the United Kingdom. They also looked at the method of lethal injection, which they likewise rejected because of its practical difficulties, but they recommended that the questions should be periodically

* The Report of the Royal Commission on Capital Punishment 1949–1953 recommends that the body shall be removed as soon as the medical officer certifies that life is extinct, and also that Press notices should be substituted for notices on the prison gates.

examined, "especially in the light of progress made in the science of anæsthetics". But it may well be that, before many such periodical examinations have taken place, capital punishment, except possibly for the crime of treason or espionage in time of war, will have become a thing of the past in this country.

I have no intention of going over the familiar ground of arguments for and against the retention of the death penalty in our penal code. But I would refer briefly to one aspect of the question which has been emphasised by three comparatively recent cases of murder. That is the possibility of an innocent person being hanged. It may be a remote possibility, but it exists and will continue to do so until human judgment becomes infallible.

During the debates in the House of Commons on the Criminal Justice Bill in 1948, Sir John Anderson, as the present Lord Waverley then was, a former Permanent Under-Secretary at the Home Office and later Home Secretary, was asked whether he could assure the House that, not going back earlier than this century, there have been no innocent men hanged. Sir John replied that he could and that to the best of his belief it was a fact. "The risk," he declared, "under the conditions as they exist in this country, of the capital penalty being executed on anyone who was not in fact guilty of the crime of which he had been convicted is so small, indeed so infinitesimal, that that consideration can be dismissed."

Personally I do not feel that it can be so dismissed. There was the notorious case of Oscar Slater, who was condemned to death in 1909 for a murder which it was subsequently shown that he did not commit. Admittedly he was reprieved, but for weeks his life hung by a thread and he spent nineteen years in prison before his innocence was conclusively established, thanks in great part to the persistence and energy of the late Sir Arthur Conan Doyle. Then there was the case of Norman Thorne, who was executed in 1925 for the murder of a girl friend. His defence was that the girl had committed suicide and that he had buried her in a panic. Three medical witnesses stated that in their opinion it was impossible for the girl's death to have taken place in the way claimed by the prosecution, and they supported the suicide theory. Yet Thorne was hanged, while the reputable *Law Journal* wrote that "Thorne's execution would leave a feeling of profound disquiet in the minds of many people".

A miscarriage of justice may also have occurred in two post-war cases. In 1947 Walter Graham Rowland was executed for the murder of a woman named Olive Balchin in a disused air-raid shelter in Manchester. The jury found Rowland guilty on the evidence before them, but they did not know that another man would later confess three times to the murder and still later withdraw his confession, eventually being charged with the attempted murder of another woman and sent to Broadmoor as a criminal lunatic. In 1950 Timothy John Evans was executed for the murder of his child. He had also been charged with the murder of his wife, which charge was not proceeded with. The principal Crown witness, John Christie, upon whose evidence Evans was convicted, later admitted it was he who had killed Mrs. Evans, in addition to other murders. At his trial Evans alleged that this was so and that Christie had killed the child as well, and though an inquiry subsequently ordered by the Home Secretary found that Evans was responsible for both deaths, the case is not free from doubt. If it had been known at the trial of Evans that the principal prosecution witness had already murdered two women, hidden their bodies temporarily in the same wash-house and had subsequently buried them in the garden, there is at least a strong likelihood, if not an absolute certainty, that Evans would have been acquitted. Nor was it possible to summon Evans to appear at the inquiry, as he had already been executed.*

No doubt errors of human judgment in murder cases have been reduced to a minimum. But, as I have tried to show, the chance of a miscarriage of justice resulting in an innocent man going to the gallows cannot be altogether ruled out. Nor am I convinced that hanging is as effective a deterrent to the potential murderer as a long term of imprisonment. I believe

* See *Hanged—and Innocent?* (1953), by R. T. Paget, Q.C., and Sydney Silverman, where these cases are carefully and authoritatively analysed.

it is only a matter of time before we follow the more enlightened example of most continental countries and relegate the hangman and the horrible tools of his trade to the barbarous past.

This book is mainly about criminals of one kind or another and about the men who prosecute, defend and try them in the courts. The earlier part I have devoted to the careers of two English lawyers whom I can only describe as eminent, and some of their cases which have particularly impressed me. Fortunately for me I have had the privilege of knowing both Sir Travers Humphreys and the late Lord Simon. Sir Travers Humphreys, alike at the Bar and on the Bench, was the most outstanding criminal practitioner of his time; he remains today the greatest authority on our criminal law. Of the many fascinating cases in which he has figured, I have chosen twelve, extending in point of time over thirty years and covering a variety of crimes such as blackmail, arson, libel, robbery and murder. Lord Simon, on the other hand, never specialised in criminal work. He covered a wider field than Sir Travers Humphreys, which eventually caused him to be regarded as the greatest all-round lawyer in the British Commonwealth. Nevertheless he did appear in a number of criminal cases, or cases with criminal associations, which are of exceptional interest. The six described here concern libel, shipwreck, espionage, the 'unwritten law', the private life of Mr. Gladstone and the biggest banknote forgery on record.

I have had something to say about other aspects of law and crime which I have felt to be of interest to the general reader as well as to those who have made a special study of criminology. Among the advocates I have written about there are Sir Patrick Hastings and Serjeant Sullivan, there is the pathologist Sir Bernard Spilsbury and there are the extraordinary cases of Ronald True, the I.R.A. saboteurs and Benjamin Bathurst, the missing diplomat. I have also dealt with different aspects of crime and criminal investigation in the United States and Soviet Russia, as well as in this country. Then there is the phenomenon of the multiple murderer, the criminal who has not been content with committing a single crime of homicide, but has gone in for murder in the mass. I have examined this peculiarly revolting type of crime, in the light of a number of remarkable cases which are not confined to the United Kingdom. Finally, I have dealt at some length with two particular types of crime, crimes of violence and juvenile crime, which I have looked at against the background of the public demand for the restoration of flogging as well as in the light of modern scientific remedial treatment.

House of Commons.
December, 1954.   H. MONTGOMERY HYDE.

I. SIR TRAVERS HUMPHREYS
AND HIS CASES

I. SIR TRAVERS HUMPHREYS AND HIS CASES

1. Sir Travers Humphreys

SIR TRAVERS HUMPHREYS, who retired from the Bench on the eve of his eighty-fourth birthday, has long been regarded as our leading judge in criminal matters. In announcing his impending retirement in 1951, Lord Goddard, the Lord Chief Justice, said that Mr. Justice Humphreys had been "a tower of strength" in the Court of Criminal Appeal and that his contribution to the criminal law of this country had been invaluable.

For more than sixty years Sir Travers was engaged in the law, mostly on its criminal side, either as advocate or judge. During this long period he has appeared in many celebrated cases. They range from that of the dramatist, Oscar Wilde, at the Old Bailey in 1895, to that of the 'acid bath' murderer, John George Haigh, at Lewes Assizes in 1949.

Sir Travers is a Londoner. He was bred to the law. His father was a solicitor, partner in one of the few firms which specialised in police court work at that time. Indeed it was through his father's influence that he was able to get away to a flying start. He received his education at Shrewsbury School and Trinity Hall, Cambridge, which has always been a great law college in the University. He was twenty-two when he was called to the Bar at the Inner Temple in 1889 and became a pupil of T. W. Chitty, then the leading 'junior' at the Common Law Bar.

Humphreys decided to concentrate on criminal work. Much of his work was necessarily conducted at the Old Bailey, where along with Sir Archibald Bodkin and the late Sir Richard Muir he may be said to have founded a new and better style of advocacy. He neither bullied nor blustered. He presented his cases without prejudice or theatrical display. All four of these traits were popular with the older school of criminal lawyer, but Humphreys would have nothing to do with any of them.

As a prosecutor he believed not that it was his duty to secure a conviction at all costs, but rather to appear as an advocate for the Crown, impartially placing before the Court all the evidence on which the jury might fairly base their verdict. As an advocate, Humphreys was much too self-controlled to let personal feelings obtrude in sensational 'scenes' in court, nor did he quarrel with the judge, as other counsel have sometimes done.

From Bodkin and Muir he learned always to be master of the facts with which he was concerned, and he never had any illusions about the strength or weakness of a particular case. Thus he was usually able to get at the truth—or rather to show the jury whether the witness was telling the truth. Indeed, he seemed to have an almost uncanny knack of getting to the heart of the matter. "Travers Humphreys always struck me as a master of his art," one of his colleagues has said. "But it all seemed quite natural—until one tried to do it oneself."

As a young barrister of only six years standing at the Bar, Humphreys first attracted public notice in the courts through the Oscar Wilde case. His father was Wilde's solicitor, and consequently he received a brief as junior counsel in the three trials in which Wilde was involved.

Humphreys has never entertained any doubt that Wilde was justly convicted. "Wilde's talents raised him almost to the level of a genius," he remarked after the case. "His mode of life dragged him down to the level of a pathological case."

Shortly after his interesting book of random jottings, *Criminal Days*, was published in 1946, I asked Sir Travers Humphreys why he had said nothing in it about the Wilde case. He told me he would have liked to do so, but that he had been unable to lay hands on any transcript of the proceedings so as to refresh his memory as to the facts in these notorious trials. Fortunately I was able to supply him with the desired material. In due course this led to an interesting collaboration between us, in which I edited an account of the trials for the 'Notable British Trials' series, while Sir Travers contributed a foreword setting out his own views on the case. This foreword was as succinct and well balanced as one of his own judgments.

Humphreys did not like Wilde personally, but he paid a well-deserved tribute to his literary abilities and to his wit as a conversationalist. He gave me an example of this, which he told me must have been wholly spontaneous on Wilde's part. It was at a conference which the barrister had with his client shortly before the first trial came on, when he told Wilde that he would be cross-examined by Edward Carson, who had been a fellow student of his in Dublin. "No doubt," remarked Wilde, "he will perform his task with all the added bitterness of an old friend."

Seven years after the Wilde case in 1902, Humphreys appeared in his first big murder case, the trial of Kitty Byron, a young dressmaker, before Mr. Justice Darling at the Old Bailey. Kitty Byron was accused of murdering her lover, a stockbroker named Reginald Baker, whom she stabbed to death on the steps of Lombard Street Post Office with a knife which she had concealed in her muff. Humphreys was her junior counsel; his leader was Sir Henry Dickens, K.C., son of the novelist. On the evidence the jury had no alternative but to find Kitty Byron guilty. However, she was reprieved. Incidentally, the funds for her defence were entirely provided by members of the Stock Exchange. They sympathised with this girl of twenty-four, who had lived with and been brutally ill-treated by Baker, a married man.

In 1905 Humphreys was appointed Treasury Counsel at the Middlesex Sessions, and three years later was promoted to the Old Bailey. He retained this position until his elevation to the Bench in 1928, thus representing the Crown in every important prosecution which took place during this period. It is an extraordinary catalogue of cases. They included Sir Roger Casement, executed for high treason; Crippen and Seddon, the poisoners; the much-married Mr. Smith, who drowned his brides in the bath; Edith Thompson and Frederick Bywaters, perhaps the most sensational love-triangle case of the century; three financiers, whom Humphreys brought to book for fraud—Ernest Terah Hooley, Horatio Bottomley and

Gerald Lee Bevan. Humphreys played an important part in sending Hawley Harvey Crippen to the scaffold in 1910. Yet he never regarded Crippen as a great villain. "He made a bad mistake and paid the penalty," Humphreys has said about this case. "In another country he would, I feel, have been given the benefit of extenuating circumstances."

It was during this period that Humphreys saw what was perhaps the most painful spectacle of his career. This was the attempt made by Frederick Henry Seddon to prevent the judge passing the death sentence. From the dock Seddon raised his hand giving a Masonic sign. The judge, who also belonged to the craft, looked down and wept as the black cap was placed on his wig. As he passed sentence he reminded Seddon that their brotherhood did not encourage crime but on the contrary condemned it.

Humphreys was the first practitioner at the Old Bailey Bar to become a High Court judge without having previously worn the silk gown of a K.C. Said his colleague, the late Sir Henry Curtis-Bennett, at the time in the Old Bailey, "We have, by the elevation of Sir Travers Humphreys to the Bench, lost a great advocate. The greatest advocate, I think, that this Court has seen for many years. But I have no doubt that the Bench and the public have gained a great judge." The truth of these words was amply proved in the succeeding years. As a judge Mr. Justice Humphreys had, of course, to try civil cases, and although his practice had taken him seldom into the civil courts, it must be admitted that he did so extraordinarily well. But he also had his meed of crime on the Bench. Among the prisoners on whom he thus sat in judgment, either as a judge alone or with his judicial brethren in the Court of Criminal Appeal, there must be mentioned Alfred Arthur Rouse, Mrs. Barney, Leopold Harris, Mrs. Rattenbury and George Stoner, Hayley Morris and the I.R.A. incendiarists. They form as remarkable a company as has fallen to the lot of any English judge to try. In the Harris fire-raising case he had the unusual experience of listening to the pleading of his barrister son Christmas Humphreys. In 1949, at the Sussex Summer Assizes, he presided, when he was eighty-two years old, with remarkable

6

skill and patience in the difficult 'acid bath' murder case of John George Haigh.

Throughout his life Humphreys has been a firm believer in the jury system, in which he has felt that the essential British sense of justice and fair play is so well embodied. No man can have addressed more juries in his time than he. It amused him when, towards the end of his career on the Bench, he received by mistake a summons to serve on one.

He had a way with him that appealed to juries—a quiet, dry humour, a pleasant laugh with a kind of cackle in it, a quick intelligence and a willingness to consider information from any source, no matter how unpromising, provided it served the ends of justice. He was sometimes a severe judge. But he has also shown great kindness and courtesy of manner. Underneath all the majesty of the law which he has personified for so long there beats a tender heart. To a man acquitted of assaulting his wife he once said with a characteristic touch, "I strongly advise you not to do it again."

Unlike some contemporaries his interests extend beyond the law. When he was eighty he still fished and played golf. He is an enthusiastic member of the Garrick Club, to which he has belonged for over forty years, and he enters with zest into the conversation and good fellowship which are always to be found within the walls of that hospitable institution. In his leisure moments he is also something of a poet. The following is the first stanza of his poem 'Long Vacation' which he composed in his eighty-fourth year.

> I think that if I had a boat
> I'd like to sail away
> From all the noise and quarrelling
> That fill the air today;
> Away from law and politics,
> From both I'd gladly part,
> From buses which will never stop
> And trains which seldom start.

Sir Travers Humphreys ended his *Criminal Days* by begging his readers' indulgence, exhorting them in the words so often addressed to every judge—but never too often—'Be Merciful'. He, who showed the quality of mercy so clearly in all his actions, both public and private, need have had no fear. His reputation as an honest, humane and dispassionate judge has been securely established with posterity, while the legacy of his example is cherished by his friends and colleagues at the Bar and on the Bench.

2. THE GREAT PEARL ROBBERY

SOME years ago Sir Travers Humphreys was invited to speak in a debate on the question, 'that Truth is stranger than Fiction'. He did so in support of the motion, giving as an illustration an amazing case of robbery in 1913 in which he helped to prosecute the thieves to conviction.

The stolen articles consisted of a world-famous necklace, consisting of sixty-one perfectly matched pearls, which had taken over ten years to collect, together with three loose pearls. The necklace was insured with Lloyd's for £130,000, but its owner, Mr. Max Mayer, a well-known diamond and pearl merchant of Hatton Garden, claimed it was worth £20,000 more than the insurance figure.

The thieves, who eventually took their places in the Old Bailey dock on November 17, 1913, were James Lockett, a professional burglar of powerful physique; Joseph Grizzard, nicknamed 'Cammi', a London Jew ostensibly trading as a diamond merchant, but known to the police as the most notorious receiver of stolen property in the country; an Austrian Jew, Simon Silverman, who traded as a diamond broker in Hatton Garden; and another Austrian Jew, Leiser Gutwirth, in the same trade in London.

The trial, which lasted for six days, took place before Mr. Justice A. T. Lawrence, afterwards Lord Trevethin. Humphreys appeared for the Crown with Sir Richard Muir, while Lockett was defended by Henry Curtis-Bennett, Grizzard by George Elliot, K.C., Silverman by J. P. Valetta and Gutwirth by Walter Frampton.

SIR TRAVERS HUMPHREYS

The story which Muir and Humphreys unfolded at the trial was indeed extraordinary. Mayer's Paris agent had sent the necklace and the three loose pearls in a sealed parcel by registered post to his principal in Hatton Garden in July of the same year. This was the usual method of consignment employed in the trade and was considered much safer and less likely to attract undesirable attention than entrusting such a packet to a special messenger.

At 9.30 on the morning of July 16, Mr. Mayer arrived in his office in Hatton Garden and found the parcel on his table. He undid it, opened the leather case in which the necklace and pearls had been packed and found, to his utter astonishment, eleven lumps of sugar wrapped in an old newspaper.

Mayer immediately informed Lloyd's underwriters and the police of the loss. By arrangement with the underwriters the police offered a reward of £10,000.

The fact that the sugar was French and the newspaper wrapping was also French at first directed suspicions towards France. But the French authorities satisfied Scotland Yard that the packet could not have been tampered with on French soil. Similar inquiries in our own postal service made it clear that nothing untoward could have happened to it in the British Post Office. How and where had the contents been abstracted?

The police, in examining the packet, noticed that it bore marks of having been opened and resealed at one end, with a die seal which was a forgery of the one used by Mayer's agent. The publication of a photograph of the packet and wax seals prompted an engraver from Hammersmith to come forward with the information that he had made the die seal for a customer, whose name he did not know. Later he was able to identify him as Silverman, when the postman who did the rounds in Hatton Garden on the morning of the theft admitted that the packet might have been in the bag which he took into the building where Silverman had his office only a few doors away from Mayer's. At Silverman's request the postman had recently been in the habit of delivering his mail to him personally, instead of handing it to the porter.

Meanwhile, a young French diamond merchant, named

D

Brandstatter, who was visiting Antwerp on business, ran into Gutwirth in the street. Gutwirth, who was distantly related to him, confessed that he had got the pearls for sale. Brandstatter returned to Paris, where he got in touch with his cousin, a young man named Quadratstein, and the two cousins decided to earn the reward offered by the police. They wrote to Gutwirth in London, who replied saying that they could have the necklace for one and a half million francs, the equivalent of £60,000.

The two young men crossed over to London and, after several preliminary meetings with Gutwirth and Silverman, were eventually taken to a house in Canonbury, where they were introduced to 'Cammi' Grizzard, who was the brains behind the robbery. Quadratstein offered half a million francs. Gutwirth refused, but agreed to take a million. A rendezvous was fixed for next day in a Lyons tea shop in Holborn for the purpose of inspecting the goods.

Soon after the two cousins arrived in the tea shop, Grizzard came in and sat down. He asked a man at the next table for a match. The man, who was the burglar Lockett, replied by tossing a match-box on to their table. Grizzard opened it to reveal three marvellous pearls, the largest of which was worth at least £10,000. The two cousins were then given a week to collect the purchase money.

The young men hurried off to Lloyd's underwriters, henceforth acting under their instructions and those of the police. A would-be buyer was now produced, a naturalised Englishman of French birth named Spanier. After several ticklish interviews with Grizzard and his confederates, who were armed, Spanier bought two of the pearls for £4,000. After further abortive meetings, it was arranged that the remainder should be handed over in return for the balance of the purchase money on September 1 at the British Museum Tube Station.

Grizzard arrived without the pearls, as he suspected a trap. Seeing no police, who were properly hidden, he arranged another meeting next morning, when he would have the pearls. He duly turned up with Lockett and Silverman, and after an exciting chase down the lift by the police, they were all arrested. Gutwirth was caught later. But no trace of the pearls could be found, either on the persons of the men or in their lodgings.

It became clear in the course of the trial that the registered packet had been carefully unsealed in Silverman's office, the jewels removed, the sugar substituted and the packet resealed with the forged die. The conspirators never expected to find a pearl necklace of fabulous price. What they hoped for was a consignment of diamonds, which they could of course have re-cut or altered to almost any shape.

All four men were found guilty, Grizzard and Lockett getting seven years penal servitude, Silverman five, and Gutwirth eighteen months imprisonment.

What happened to the pearls? A piano-back maker named Horn was walking along St. Paul's Road, Finsbury, about a fortnight after the arrests, when he saw a match-box lying in the gutter. He picked it up and found the pearls inside. The matchbox had been thrown there by Lockett's wife, apparently in the hopes it would be discovered by the police.

But the police in the local station, to whom Horn reported his find, thought that the pearls were imitation, and sent them to the Lost Property Office in Scotland Yard. Here their true value was appreciated, and, in the result, all but two of the original pearls were restored to their owner.

No wonder the famous Lutine bell was rung at Lloyd's when the news became known there.

3. THE BUTTON AND BADGE MURDER

IN the early morning of Sunday, February 10, 1918, the body of a girl was discovered on Eltham Common near Woolwich, a few yards from the main road. Soon a curious crowd of sightseers collected, which attracted the attention of a passing tram-driver. He reported the incident to the police and drove on. The police were promptly on the scene and had no difficulty in identifying the body as that of Nellie Grace True, aged sixteen, whose father, an employee in the

Woolwich Arsenal, had already reported her disappearance.

On the previous evening she had gone out to change a book at the Plumstead library. Usually when changing a book she returned about nine, but as there was no sign of her at that hour her father had first thought she might have gone to a cinema. At midnight he gave the alarm. The police doctor who examined the body stated that the girl had first been overpowered and then strangled, apparently with bare hands. When the body had been removed and the crowd was beginning to disperse, one of the onlookers handed the constable in charge a plain round button of the size used on overcoats. It was made of bone, and through two of its holes went a piece of metal wire, one end of which had been sharpened and the other broken off.

The policeman, on being shown the place where this was found, noticed that the ground bore signs of a struggle having taken place there. A little further away he saw another object in the mud, which he picked up. It looked like a military badge and represented a tiger. These were the only clues pointing to the identity of the murderer. Yet within barely two months a man stood in the dock at the Old Bailey charged with the murder of Nellie True.

At the trial, which took place on April 26, 1918, the man was prosecuted by Sir Travers Humphreys. Mr. Justice Atkin was on the Bench.

The story which Humphreys set out constituted a remarkable example of the weight of circumstantial evidence. The badge, on close examination, had proved to be a cheap replica of the badge of the Leicestershire Regiment, such as was worn by those interested in (as distinct from belonging to) the regiment. As for the button, the wire attached to it was found to be spring steel of a peculiar make. It looked as if the button might have been fastened to an overcoat by this wire instead of by thread.

The police also deduced that the two articles belonged to the same individual; that at the time this individual was wearing a civilian overcoat, though he had been interested in the Leicestershire Regiment; that he was familiar with metal working and had probably been employed in a munition factory where this type of wire was in use.

At the same time the police had the articles photographed and the pictures sent to all the newspapers in the hope that publication would induce the owner to come forward and claim them.

This move met with a rapid response. Two men called at Tottenham Court Road Police Station. One of them, David Greenwood, was a youth of twenty-one, who had been discharged from the Army with shellshock after three years' service and was then working in a factory near Oxford Street engaged in the production of airplane parts. He said he thought the badge might be his, as he had worn one like it as a memento of his war service when he was attached to the Leicestershires. But, according to his account, he had sold it to a civilian whom he met in a tramcar during the week-end in which Nellie True was killed.

The other man was a work-mate of Greenwood's who had brought the newspaper pictures to his notice. "It looks uncommonly like the one you were wearing," he said to him. Another work-mate, who was standing by, suggested that Greenwood ought to go to the police 'and clear the matter up'. Greenwood reluctantly agreed to do this.

Greenwood was then asked to come to Scotland Yard and make a formal statement. On the way there in the police car the inspector noticed that Greenwood's overcoat was entirely devoid of buttons. He asked Greenwood the reason.

"They have been off for a long time," was the reply.

On looking more closely, the inspector saw that in most of the gaps there were threads as if the buttons had been torn off, but that in the bottom one there were no threads—only a jagged hole. What was Greenwood's explanation of that?

"That is where it was pulled out, I suppose," he replied.

In the inspector's room in Scotland Yard the button and badge were openly displayed on a desk. Without saying a word, the inspector picked up the button and placed it in the hole in Greenwood's overcoat. It fitted perfectly.

The inspector was convinced that Greenwood was the guilty

man. But he now had the task of proving it. Leaving Green-wood at the Yard, he immediately went to the factory in Oxford Street and questioned the other employees.

They all said that Greenwood had worn his coat buttoned during the few days before the murder. One workmate, in particular stated—and subsequently repeated it in the witness box—that Greenwood had the badge on his coat when the men stopped work on the Saturday, but was not wearing it on the following Monday morning.

It only remained to identify the wire. The inspector picked up several pieces in the factory and then sent for the manager.

He placed them in a row together with the piece found in the button and asked the manager to pick out which of them came from the factory. "All of them," was the answer.

The works foreman, separately examined, gave a similar reply.

Greenwood was then arrested and charged with the murder. He would not admit his guilt, but made a statement about his movements on the Saturday. He said he had been at home from 7 to 9.45 p.m., that he had then visited the Y.M.C.A. hostel in Woolwich for supper, had stayed there till eleven, when he caught the last tram home and had then gone straight to bed. According to his statement, he had not had a button on his coat for several weeks since his mother was ill and there was no one else at home to sew them on again.

For the prosecution Humphreys called Sir Bernard Spilsbury, the pathologist, as an expert witness to the time and manner of the girl's death. Sir Bernard, who had carried out a post-mortem, said that she must have died not later than 2 a.m., probably earlier, that death was due to asphyxia from strangulation—there were marks caused by pressure of fingers on her neck—and that she had obviously offered considerable resistance to the assault.

Mr. Henry Slesser, for the defence, asked Spilsbury how a man who had been discharged from the Army with shellshock and neurasthenia could have committed such a crime. Spilsbury could not say. But Humphreys later pointed out that the prisoner had had six months in which to recover from a condition which would tend to improve under normal conditions of life.

Greenwood left the dock for the witness-box to give evidence on his own behalf. He stuck to his story of selling the badge to a stranger and denied all knowledge of the crime. Cross-examined by Humphreys as to what had become of his buttons he said he had used them to pack a lathe. Humphreys then proceeded to demonstrate the absurdity of using anything so fragile as bone buttons to pack a metal lathe.

After an absence of three hours the jury found Greenwood guilty, but added a strong recommendation to mercy on account of his youth and war service. Asked by the judge whether he had anything to say, Greenwood reiterated his innocence—and surprisingly asked the judge to disregard the recommendation to mercy. "Rather than have the disgrace of the crime on me," he said, "I would pay the full penalty."

The judge observed that in spite of what the prisoner had said, he would forward the recommendation to the proper quarter where, no doubt, it would receive every consideration. It did. On the eve of his execution, the capital sentence was commuted to one of penal servitude for life.

One thing is certain. There were no doubts in the mind of Sir Travers Humphreys that this reprieve was entirely due to the jury's recommendation to mercy and not to any dissatisfaction with the justice of their verdict.

4. THE BLACK BOOK TRIAL

HORATIO BOTTOMLEY was not the only M.P. prosecuted by Sir Travers Humphreys. There was also the eccentric Mr. Noel Pemberton Billing, who represented Mid-Hertfordshire as an Independent during the 1914–1918 War. He was charged with criminally libelling a well-known dancer of the time named Maud Allan and the theatrical producer J. T. Grein. The case, which centred around her part in his production of Oscar Wilde's celebrated play *Salome*, afterwards came to be known as the Black Book Trial.

At the time of the trial Pemberton Billing was in his late thirties. He usually wore a monocle and a long pointed collar without the usual accompaniment of a necktie, and he used to drive about in a light yellow Rolls-Royce. He had been, in his time, a sailor, inventor and actor, and was one of the first Englishmen to realise the possibilities of aircraft, particularly in future wars. As a young man, he had actually designed an airplane which flew. In 1916, when he entered Parliament, he pledged himself to support a strong air policy and a more vigorous conduct of the war generally. He founded a weekly newspaper called *The Imperialist*, which was issued to subscribers only.

Unfortunately, Mr. Pemberton Billing's patriotic feelings carried him to extravagant lengths. The issue of *The Imperialist* for January 26, 1918, carried an extraordinary leading article from his pen, entitled 'As I See It—the First 47,000'. It dealt with a book supposed to have been compiled by the German Secret Service from reports of its agents in Britain, and to be in possession of a certain German prince. This so-called Black Book was alleged to contain the names of no fewer than 47,000 Britons whose sexual vices were known to the Germans, who could thus blackmail them.

It may seem incredible that people should have believed such rubbish, but many people believed in its existence, for in the popular mood of war hysteria which prevailed at the time anything was possible. Some months previously a society had been formed called The Vigilantes with the object of promoting 'purity in public life', and to some extent *The Imperialist* had become the organ of this society. At the beginning of February, 1918, Pemberton Billing changed the title of his paper to *The Vigilante*, to mark its association with that movement, whose members all believed wholeheartedly in the existence of the Black Book.

About the same time an event was announced in London's theatrical world. This was the presentation of two private performances by Mr. J. T. Grein's Independent Theatre Society of Wilde's *Salome*—a work which had previously come under the ban of the Lord Chamberlain. For the name part Mr,

Grein had secured Miss Maud Allan, whose dancing had previously created something of a sensation. She had dispensed with more clothing than some people considered proper on the stage. In this production she was to give 'the dance of the seven veils'.

On February 16, 1918, the first number of *The Vigilante* contained the following paragraph, written by Mr. Pemberton Billing:

THE CULT OF THE——

To be a member of Maud Allan's private performances in Oscar Wilde's *Salome* one has to apply to a Miss Valetta, of 9, Duke Street, Adelphi, W.C. If Scotland Yard were to seize the list of these members I have no doubt they would secure the names of several thousand of the first 47,000.

The last word of the heading is not given. But it contained some of the sting of the libel, constituting, as it did, an allusion to sexual perversity. As Sir Travers Humphreys said in opening the case for the prosecution at Bow Street Police Court, "A more horrible libel to publish of any woman, in my submission, it is impossible to find."

It was not long before this offensive paragraph reached the notice of Miss Allan and Mr. Grein. The libel was sufficiently grave to justify criminal proceedings and for this reason they were able to obtain leave from the High Court to institute a private prosecution against the writer. Mr. Pemberton Billing was accordingly arrested, and after Humphreys had outlined the case against him in the police court he was committed for trial at the next Old Bailey sessions.

The trial was probably marked by more disorderly scenes than have ever been witnessed on any similar occasion at the Old Bailey. This was largely due to Billing's decision to conduct his own defence, a proceeding which gained him the well-merited description by Humphreys as "a gentleman who thinks he knows more law than anyone else". The atmosphere was further heated by his antagonism to the presiding judge, Mr. Justice Darling, to whose presence on the Bench Pemberton Billing violently, but unsuccessfully, objected.

The late Sir Ellis Hume-Williams, K.C., was brought in to lead Humphreys for the prosecution. After Miss Allan had identified herself as the person referred to in the libel, Pemberton Billing began his defence and called a string of witnesses whose evidence in no way justified the libel. Some of them deposed to having seen the Black Book. Others sought to prove that *Salome* was an immoral play.

A young woman who gave her name as Mrs. Eileen Villiers Stuart electrified the court by reciting some of the names in the book which, she said, she had seen. They included Mr. and Mrs. Asquith, Lord Haldane and, surprisingly enough, Mr. Justice Darling himself.

Most startling of the so-called expert witnesses was Lord Alfred Douglas, who was called as the former friend of Wilde and translator of his play, which had originally been written in French. Oscar Wilde, he thought, was "the greatest force for evil that has appeared in Europe during the last 350 years". He intensely regretted having met him and helped him with the translation, which he now regarded as "a most pernicious and abominable piece of work".

"What has all this to do with the character of Miss Maud Allan?" asked the judge.

"I have nothing to say against the private character of Miss Allan," replied Mr. Pemberton Billing.

The concluding stages of this remarkable trial were heard in an atmosphere alternating between intermittent uproar and *opera bouffe*. The judge announced he had received numerous anonymous letters, while it was said that Mrs. Villiers Stuart had been threatened that if she went into the witness-box again she would be shot from the gallery. Pemberton Billing openly accused the judge of bullying him, for which he was promptly threatened with committal for contempt of court.

The judge summed up to a background of cheering, hissing and other interruptions. People were removed from court one after another. Lord Alfred Douglas, who objected to what Darling said about his contribution to *Salome*, shouted wildly as he was being ushered out, "You have no right to say that

I wrote it. You lie. You are a damned liar. If you say it
outside the court I will prosecute you."

To do him justice, the judge did his best to disabuse the
minds of the jury that they were trying Oscar Wilde and his
play. But it was no use. After an absence of an hour and a
half the foreman announced their verdict—not guilty.

Tumultuous cheering broke out, which the judge was helpless to silence and which continued for several minutes. The
ovation was repeated by the crowds outside when Pemberton
Billing emerged a free man. But for the unprecedented temper
of the times, it seems safe to say that he would not have done so.

Perhaps the most pathetic figure in this trial was Maud Allan.
Pemberton Billing had admitted that he had nothing against
her private character. She was therefore entitled to have the
issue plainly put to the jury as to whether the paragraph in the
paper constituted a libel upon her. It was never so put.

"Poor Miss Allan," remarked Sir Travers Humphreys in
recalling the case many years later. "She had little cause to love
the law or, should I say, the administration of it."

5. THE CASE OF THE FORGED TELEGRAMS

AN ingenious trick practised on a number of bookmakers
formed the basis of an interesting case in which Sir Travers
Humphreys was concerned as prosecutor at the Old Bailey in
March, 1922. The case attracted much attention at the time,
not only on account of the remarkable facts which it disclosed,
but also by reason of the prominent social position of the two
defendants involved. This was the trial of Captain Owen Peel,
twenty-eight-year-old former Guards officer, and his wife, Mrs.
Violet Margaret Florence Peel, on charges of obtaining money
from bookmakers by means of forged telegrams.

As is well known, starting-price bookmakers have arrangements with their clients by which telegraphed bets on horses
are accepted up to agreed amounts even if the telegrams reach
their offices after the race has been run. But it is, of course,
an essential part of the arrangement that the telegrams must

be handed in to the post office before the start of the race.

The substance of the charges against Captain and Mrs. Peel was that they ascertained the name of the winner of a particular race and inserted it in telegrams addressed to bookmakers after the race was over whilst making it appear that these bets had in fact been despatched before the 'off'. The race in question was the Duke of York's Handicap, which was run at Kempton Park on October 8, 1921, and was won by a horse named Paragon.

At the relevant date the Peels were living in the little village of Aston Dassett in Oxfordshire. The village shop also served as the local post and telegraph office, and all its business was conducted by the elderly owner and a young girl assistant. On the day of the race, which was a Saturday, the girl went off for the afternoon to a sale of work in the near-by vicarage.

The handicap was due to start at 2.50. A few minutes before this time Captain Peel and his wife entered the shop. Mrs. Peel told the shopkeeper that she was expecting a telephone call from London at any moment. At the same time her husband handed in a telegram for despatch. This was addressed to a private individual and had nothing to do with betting.

At 2.52 precisely Mrs. Peel's call came through from London and she spoke to the caller on the line. While she was doing so Captain Peel watched the shopkeeper marking the time at which his telegram was handed in. The man put this at 2.50, but Captain Peel suggested that 2.45 would be more accurate, and the change was duly made. He then waited for his wife to finish her conversation. The shopkeeper also waited with the telegram in his hand, since it had to be telephoned to Banbury, and this could not be done until Mrs. Peel had finished, there being only one line out of the post office.

Now it so happened that the Kempton Park race was ten minutes late starting. It took about two minutes to run, and the name of the winner was known in London a minute later. A few moments afterwards Mrs. Peel still on the telephone, beckoned to her husband, and he went over and stood beside her for several moments with his back to the shopkeeper. During this brief period his wife said something to him.

Captain Peel then went to the door of the shop as if to leave, but stopped and turning round said to the shopkeeper, "Oh, I'd almost forgotten these. He thereupon produced no less than forty-five telegrams from his pocket. They were addressed to bookmakers all over the country backing Paragon both for win and place. Most of these telegrams were signed by him, although eight bore the signature of his wife.

It was five-past three when Mrs. Peel completed her telephone conversation, which had lasted for thirteen minutes. She immediately left the shop to return home. Captain Peel remained behind while the shopkeeper went off to the vicarage to fetch his young assisant to deal with the bundle of telegrams. When the girl arrived she inserted the time of despatch as 2.45, being given to understand by Captain Peel that they had been handed in at the same time as the first one. She then went to the telephone and began to transmit them to Banbury. After the telegraph clerk in Banbury Post Office had taken down the texts of two of the telegrams, he asked the girl if the timing was correct, since it was now 3.30. She checked this again with Captain Peel, who assured her that it was and she passed on this assurance to Banbury. It was nearly four o'clock when the last of the telegrams was despatched.

Though the bookmakers were surprised to receive what appeared to be genuine winning bets on a race so long after it was over, most of them paid up without question. As a result Captain Peel got over £2,000 in winnings. But one firm of bookmakers was suspicious and asked the post office to make inquiries. An official from the G.P.O. in London went down to Aston Dassett and after interviewing the various parties concerned reported to the Postmaster-General, who decided to institute criminal proceedings against the Peels.

In the Old Bailey trial which followed, Sir Charles Gill and Sir Travers Humphreys appeared for the Crown, while the captain and his wife were defended by Sir Henry Curtis-Bennett, K.C., and Sir Richard Muir. The presiding judge was Mr. Justice Darling.

At the preliminary police court proceedings the prosecution had suggested that the sequence of events in the village shop had been deliberately engineered by Captain Peel. In other words, that he had learned the name of the winner from his wife after the horse had passed the post and had then inserted it in the telegraph forms which were already prepared. When he came up at the Old Bailey Captain Peel made no attempt to deny this. Accordingly, he pleaded guilty.

Mrs. Peel, however, decided to plead not guilty on the advice of her counsel. Their view was that as the law then stood a wife accused of committing a crime was presumed to be acting under her husband's coercion and was therefore entitled to an acquittal. Mrs. Peel's defence in fact, as apart from in law, was contained in a document which Sir Travers Humphreys read out in court and on which she was later cross-examined. This took the form of a statement made by her to the G.P.O. official who first investigated the case. In this statement she declared that her telephone call in the post office was concerned with Stock Exchange transactions and had nothing to do with racing. She admitted that eight of the telegrams were in her handwriting, but denied that the name of the winner had been subsequently written in.

On the point of law the judge upheld the principle that, under the common law of England for nearly thirteen centuries, a wife who committed a crime in the presence of her husband was presumed, except in certain rare instances, to act under his compulsion. This principle, he observed, was presumably based on the assumption that wives could not contradict their husbands, which seemed to be contrary to the present-day fact. Mr. Justice Darling added that in his opinion this legal protection afforded to married women was absolutely inappropriate to modern life, seeing that under recent legislation they could be J.P.s, serve on juries and be elected to Parliament. However, such was the law, and he had no alternative but to direct the jury to return a verdict of not guilty in the case of Mrs. Peel.

Incidentally, this trial was marked by a noteworthy display of judicial ignorance on the part of the judge. For instance, he had to ask Sir Travers Humphreys what constituted an 'each way' bet of £2. "I do not know what it means," he remarked amid laughter. "I have read of a person who thought it meant £2 if a horse won and £2 if it did not."

As soon as Mrs. Peel had been discharged her husband stepped into the dock to receive sentence. Mr. Justice Darling sent him to prison for twelve months. It was doubtless unlucky for him that the start of the race was delayed for ten minutes and that the shopkeeper's assistant in the local post office was away at the vicarage. Otherwise the fraud might well have succeeded since the telephone conversation would have been very short and the telegrams would have reached the book-makers much sooner than they actually did.

One noteworthy feature of this trial, in which Sir Travers Humphreys helped to prosecute, was that it led to a significant change in the law. By the Criminal Justice Act 1925, coercion is now no longer automatically presumed where a wife commits an offence jointly with her husband and in his presence. Today the onus rests upon her to prove actual coercion before she can be acquitted.

6. THE END OF HORATIO BOTTOMLEY

ONE of Sir Travers Humphreys's greatest successes in the courts was his feat of laying that arch-rogue Horatio Bottomley by the heels. The occasion was Bottomley's conviction in 1922 of the fraudulent conversion to his own purposes of more than £250,000 of moneys received by him from members of the public for investment in the Government Victory Loan.

As a youth, Horatio was a shorthand reporter in the Law Courts, where he acquired considerable legal learning as well as forensic skill, which distinguished him for much of his chequered career. He later became a company promoter, whose companies failed regularly, and he also posed as a political philanthropist, which incidentally helped to secure his return as M.P. for South Hackney. During the 1914–18 War he conducted a spectacular recruiting campaign. For many years Bottomley pretended to be the illegitimate son of Charles Bradlaugh, whom he somewhat resembled. Actually his father was a tailor's foreman who ended his life as a lunatic, while his mother was a sister of Bradlaugh's friend, George Holyoake, the founder of the Co-operative Movement

In all he was prosecuted four times. Three of the cases resulted in acquittal. It was the fourth, in which Humphreys prosecuted, that led to his undoing.

When the Government floated its Victory Loan after the 1914–18 War, the smallest bonds were of a nominal value of £5, issued at £4 5s. Bottomley conceived the brilliant idea of forming a club, so that the 'little man' and the 'little woman' could share in the loan by subscribing smaller sums with the accumulation of which Bottomley would buy Victory Bonds. Interest on the club's holding of stocks and bonuses, represented by the Government's annual redemptions, were to be combined in a fund which would be distributed by lot among the subscribers, who would also be entitled to withdraw their subscriptions at any time and get their money back in full. Bottomley now invited the public to subscribe in units of 15s. 6d., representing the purchase price of a £1 share, the proceeds of which he undertook to incorporate in the 'Victory Bond Club'.

The public fell for the scheme in a big way. Between June 17, 1919, and the end of the year Bottomley received subscriptions to the amount of nearly half a million pounds. Some of this had gone to the Treasury, but much of it had been dishonestly applied by Bottomley to various companies or else barefacedly transferred to his own pocket. In 1921 the Official Receiver took over the affairs of the club, and early in the following year Bottomley received summonses to appear at Bow Street Police Court.

Sir Travers Humphreys was entrusted with the conduct of the prosecution. Since an M.P. was involved, the normal practice would have been for the Crown to be represented by one of the Law Officers, as Humphreys pointed out at the time; but such was the legend of Bottomley's invincibility that Mr. Lloyd George's Government, which was highly nervous about the proceedings, declined to instruct the Attorney- or Solicitor-General for this purpose. However, they offered

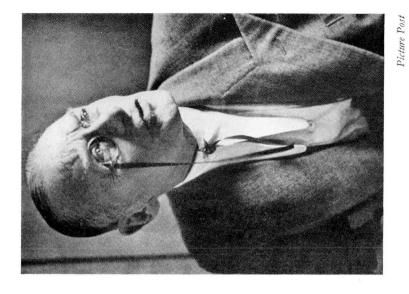

Noel Pemberton-Billing, M.P.

Horatio Bottomley

EDITH THOMPSON

FREDERICK BYWATERS

Humphreys any K.C. he chose to lead him, but Humphreys refused this offer. Though he had no special knowledge of accountancy, he put aside all other work to prepare the case, had an extra table brought into his chambers in the Temple, and worked for weeks with the accountants, so that he eventually knew the crooked figures as well as Bottomley himself.

The truth was that Bottomley's dissipated habits had made him careless. "I have been lauded as having done something wonderful in getting Bottomley convicted," Sir Travers Humphreys has said. "In truth it was not I who floored Bottomley, it was drink. The man I met in 1922 was a drink-sodden creature, whose brain could only be got to work by repeated doses of champagne."

The case began at Bow Street on March 8, 1922. On his way to the court Bottomley waylaid Humphreys's clerk and asked for a few minutes interview with his master. Humphreys consented, provided his junior, the late H. D. Roome, was present.

Bottomley asked two favours at the interview. First, he wanted a short adjournment each day at 11.30, so that he could have a pint of champagne, which he could not do without. He would call it his 'medicine' to the magistrate. Humphreys agreed, provided the magistrate had no objection. Secondly, Bottomley wanted Humphreys to suppress the name of a certain lady into whose account, which he had opened for her in the same bank, he had paid various Victory Loan subscriptions. Humphreys agreed provided that Bottomley would state that the account was his own private one. If there was any attempt at prevarication the lady would be put into the witness-box.

Bottomley, as was his habit, conducted his own defence. The tactics pursued by Humphreys were, by the remorseless cross-examination of the accused and his witnesses, to nullify the effect of any emotional appeal to the jury which Bottomley might make.

For instance, one of Bottomley's witnesses was questioned about shares in the Plumpton racecourse he had sold to

Bottomley. "You don't think I paid for those shares with stolen money?" Bottomley asked him. "I would not have sold them to you if I thought anything of the kind," replied the virtuous witness.

Humphreys immediately displayed this answer in its true light when he rose to cross-examine.

"Did you know where the money came from?" he asked.

"No," said the witness.

Bottomley was committed for trial, and three weeks later he took his place in the dock at the Old Bailey. Humphreys again led the prosecution. "I never felt the slightest doubt as to the result of the case," he said afterwards. "In fact the only people who were really fascinated or terrified by the rascal were the politicians in the House of Commons, a much more impressionable and, to my thinking, less reliable body of persons than an Old Bailey jury."

In less than half an hour the jury found Bottomley guilty on twenty-three counts in the indictment. Mr. Justice Salter thereupon sentenced him to seven years penal servitude.

He tried one or two journalistic ventures when he came out of prison, but completely failed to regain any measure of public confidence or esteem. He then retired to obscurity, falling into such reduced circumstances that he eventually applied for the Old Age Pension.

Bottomley was a man of exceptional talents, but when he faced Travers Humphreys from the dock in 1922, he knew his number was up. The last time Sir Travers saw him was in the bar on Ostend racecourse, after his release, still drinking champagne, but obviously at the end of his tether. He died not long afterwards. "What a wasted life," was Humphreys's comment.

"What a pity!"

7. THE THOMPSON-BYWATERS MURDER

THE discovery of a series of letters, written by an infatuated housewife to her lover, was the means of placing the woman in the dock at the Old Bailey on a capital charge in one of the most remarkable trials of this century. Sir Travers Humphreys helped to prosecute in this case, which involved the guilty lover as well as the woman, and which aroused intense public interest at the time. It later formed the theme of two successful plays, originally banned by the Lord Chamberlain—*People Like Us*, by the late Frank Vosper, and *A Pin to See a Peepshow*, by Miss Tennyson Jesse.

The scene begins late on the night of October 3, 1922. Percy Thompson, a thirty-two-year-old shipping clerk, was returning with his wife, Edith, to their home in Ilford, after visiting a London theatre. The wife, aged twenty-eight, worked as a book-keeper with a firm of milliners in Aldersgate Street. They had been somewhat unhappily married for seven years and had no children. Each earned £6 a week. They left the house at 8.15 in the morning and returned about 7 o'clock in the evening, except on occasional nights out such as this. As they were walking along Belgrave Road towards Kensington Gardens, Ilford, where they lived, suddenly a man jumped out of the shadows. Seizing Thompson by the arm, he said, "Why don't you get a divorce from your wife, you cad?"

"I've got her. I'll keep her, and I'll shoot you," replied Thompson.

Thereupon the other man pulled out a knife, with which he stabbed the husband several times, eventually killing him with a thrust at the back of the neck.

"Oh, don't! Oh, don't!" shouted Mrs. Thompson, as the attacker ran off. A few moments later Thompson collapsed and died on the pavement.

Mrs. Thompson told the police that a strange man had attacked her husband. But she did not mention that words had passed between them nor that she knew the assailant. The police then questioned the dead man's brother, who told them that, some time before, a ship's steward named Frederick Bywaters had made trouble between husband and wife.

Bywaters was later traced to the home of Mrs. Thompson's parents, and since there were bloodstains on his coat, he was taken to Ilford police station and detained. In a suitcase at his mother's house a bundle of letters was found. They had been written to him by Edith Thompson. As a result of this find Mrs. Thompson was also arrested.

Neither she nor Bywaters knew that the other was at the police station. Then a curious incident occurred. As she was led past a window she saw her lover sitting inside under arrest. "Oh, God, why did he do it?" she cried. "I didn't want him to do it." She then confessed that it was Bywaters who had killed her husband.

Bywaters subsequently admitted that he had struck the fatal blow, behaving rather more creditably than his mistress, whom he now did his best to shield. He insisted that Mrs. Thompson knew nothing of his intention to waylay her husband on their homeward journey, and he stuck to this story at the trial.

Further letters from Edith Thompson to Bywaters were found in his ship, and these appeared to show that not only did she desire to murder her husband, but that she had herself at various times tried to kill him with powdered glass and various poisons. She was, therefore, indicted jointly with Bywaters on the charge of murdering Percy Thompson.

Sir Travers Humphreys was entrusted with the prosecution, although when the case reached the Old Bailey on December 6, 1922, the Solicitor-General, Sir Thomas Inskip, later Lord Caldecote, appeared to lead him. Bywaters was defended by Mr. Cecil Whiteley, K.C., and Mrs. Thompson by Sir Henry Curtis-Bennett, K.C. The presiding judge was Mr. Justice Shearman.

Bywaters, who was eight years younger than Mrs. Thompson, was an attractive, virile youth with little or no imagination. His mistress, on the other hand, suffered from an excess of imagination, living in a world of tawdry romance and fantastic make-believe. While he was away for long periods at sea, she would write him letters, described by Mr. Justice Shearman as 'gush', in which she set out her actions and thoughts in revealing detail. 'Darlingest', contracted to 'darlint', was her favourite term of endearment for her lover.

It is the curious passion breathed by these letters, which depict the writer as half mother and half slave-mistress, that makes them of such absorbing interest. In one letter she wrote:

> Yes, darlint, you are jealous of *him*—but I want you to be —he has the right by law to all that you have the right by nature and love—yes, darlint, be jealous, so much that you will do something desperate.

Among the cuttings from newspapers enclosed with this letter was one referring to a death due to broth made from a chicken which had eaten rat poison. Other cuttings contained such headings as 'The Poisoner Curate', 'Poisoned Chocolates', 'Masterful Men' and 'Woman the Consoler'.

Many of the letters contained passages of actual beauty, which one would not have expected in a person of Mrs. Thompson's modest literary attainments. They were read out in court by Sir Travers Humphreys, in tones described by an onlooker as "by no means unsympathetic".

Both the accused gave evidence on their own behalf. Bywaters's case was that he was acting in self-defence, but it hardly bears scrutiny, particularly as he admitted, in cross-examination, that he was the aggressor and that his victim was unarmed at the time.

Edith Thompson's defence, scarcely more plausible, was that she deliberately deceived her lover into thinking that she wanted to poison her husband, but that she had no intention of putting the deception into practice. She did this, she said, because she wanted to keep Bywaters's love.

The jury found both prisoners guilty, and they were sentenced to death. They parted for the last time in the dock. Appeals were subsequently lodged, but these were dismissed by the Court of Criminal Appeal. Neither would the Home Secretary intervene, although he received petitions for Mrs. Thompson's reprieve bearing many thousands of signatures from all over the country.

They were both hanged at the same hour in different prisons on January 9, 1923. The man met his end with apparent unconcern; she was assisted to the scaffold in a state bordering on collapse.

Many have thought that Mrs. Thompson should not have been executed. She was, of course, convicted by reason of the incriminating passages contained in her letters, and these made it clear beyond doubt that she designed to encompass her husband's death in some way. Humphreys personally did not think there was any miscarriage of justice either in her case or in that of Bywaters, and I agree with him.

The murder was the consequence of frustrated passion, since the lovers had little opportunity of meeting except in tea shops and for walks in municipal parks. Had they belonged to a more leisured class, nothing would ever have been heard of them except possibly in the Divorce Court.

8. THE MR. 'A' CASE

SOON after he became Chief Senior Treasury Counsel, Sir Travers Humphreys was instructed to prosecute in one of the most sensational cases which occurred in the years between the two world wars. This was the trial in 1925 of William Cooper Hobbs, an elderly solicitor's clerk, for blackmailing Sir Hari Singh, the wealthy heir to the throne of Kashmir and, later, its Maharajah. Hobbs and two other men were charged with conspiring to blackmail Sir Hari. But neither of the two other accused men was in custody. One of them, Sir Hari's A.D.C., Captain Charles Arthur, was in a French gaol awaiting trial on a similar charge. The other was a plausible scoundrel and forger named Montague Noel Newton, who had turned King's Evidence so as to bear witness against his confederates. The presiding judge was Mr. Justice Avory.

Sir Travers Humphreys related an amazing story when he opened the case against Hobbs at the Old Bailey. It began at the Victory Ball which was held at the Albert Hall on the first anniversary of the Armistice. Sir Hari Singh had taken a box for the evening. As sometimes happens on these occasions, he struck up a conversation with a charming and attractive woman in the next box. Her name was Mrs. Robinson and she was the wife of a bookmaker, Charles Ernest Robinson.

A strong friendship soon developed between the Indian potentate and the bookmaker's wife. They spent a great deal of time in each other's company and made several trips abroad, including one to Paris. It was there that the most dramatic incident occurred in their relations.

One morning while Sir Hari Singh and Mrs. Robinson were in their hotel together, the bedroom door was flung open and an Englishman suddenly appeared saying, "Now I've got the evidence I want."

Sir Hari was naturally distressed at this unexpected caller, the more so as he immediately gained the impression that the Englishman was Mrs. Robinson's husband. Actually he was nothing of the sort. The man was Newton, who had previously made Mrs. Robinson his mistress and then blackmailed her.

Sir Hari was extremely shaken, and his anxiety was increased when his A.D.C., Captain Arthur, came to him and reported that Mr. Robinson was preparing to divorce his wife and would cite him as co-respondent. The A.D.C., who was also in the plot, pointed out that such a scandal might well result in Sir Hari being deprived of his succession to the Kashmir throne. The upshot was that Sir Hari made out a cheque for £150,000 and gave it to Arthur to take to Robinson's solicitors in consideration of their client's withdrawing divorce proceedings.

Mr. Robinson, it appeared, had previously been approached by Newton, who told him that his wife was misconducting herself with an Indian in Paris. He then let himself be taken by Newton, not to his usual solicitors, but to another firm whose managing clerk was William Cooper Hobbs. Hobbs agreed to handle the divorce proceedings on Robinson's behalf. Shortly afterwards, however, he told both Mr. and Mrs. Robinson that Sir Hari Singh was prepared to pay £25,000 to escape divorce proceedings, and the Robinsons agreed to accept this sum as a compromise. Hobbs then deducted £4,000 to cover his 'fees' and handed over the balance to Mrs. Robinson.

The same day Newton arrived in Mrs. Robinson's flat and took from her by force £10,000 of the sum she had received from Hobbs. The remaining £11,000 Robinson allowed his wife to keep. He also forgave her infidelity and they became reconciled.

A year or two later Mr. Robinson happened to meet Captain Arthur and learned from him that the hush money paid by his employer was not £25,000 but £150,000, and, moreover, this amount had been paid into a branch of the Midland Bank in Robinson's name. Robinson then went to the bank and found to his surprise that not only was this so but the money had been paid out again to someone who had presented a cheque purporting to bear Robinson's signature. As the signature was obviously forged, Robinson asked the bank to pay him the sum. But the bank refused and Robinson brought an action against it.

In these proceedings Newton, who gave evidence for the bank, swore that it was Hobbs who had endorsed the cheque.

The jury found: (1) That a conspiracy had existed, but that the Robinsons were innocent of any share in it; (2) That the bank, in paying out the money, had obeyed the mandate which it had received from the depositor. The judge ruled that this was a verdict for the bank.

Hobbs was arrested immediately afterwards as he was boarding a ship at Gravesend for Rotterdam. Throughout the action against the bank Sir Hari Singh had been referred to as 'Mr. A', but when Hobbs was charged his identity was revealed.

In opening the case against Hobbs at the Old Bailey Sir Travers Humphreys said that, since the jury in a civil court had acquitted Mr. and Mrs. Robinson of any share in the conspiracy to blackmail Sir Hari, he would present the case on that assumption. This he proceeded to do, although the judge remarked that the verdict of a civil jury is in no way binding in a criminal court.

Newton was the principal witness against Hobbs. The prosecution, said Humphreys, would have greatly liked to see him in the dock beside the prisoner, but unfortunately Hobbs's guilt could not be established without this evidence. Consequently Newton furnished all the details already described.

Hobbs gave evidence on his own behalf. He was a sick man and more than once had to be removed from court for medical attention. He also cut a sorry figure in the witness-box, particularly when being cross-examined by Humphreys. "Is it your case," Humphreys began, "that there was no conspiracy to defraud Sir Hari Singh?"

"It seems to me now that there was," Hobbs answered, "but I was no party to it."

Hobbs added that he honestly thought, when he wrote solicitor's letters to Sir Hari, that Newton was Mrs. Robinson's husband.

Humphreys neatly countered this assertion by forcing Hobbs to admit that he had been a witness at Newton's marriage some time before to another lady.

Question after question showed that Hobbs was much too shrewd to be so easily deceived by Newton, whom he had known intimately for a long time.

Of Hobbs's guilt, Humphreys told the jury there could be no doubt. Both he and Newton knew very well that whoever put Robinson's signature on the back of the cheque for £150,000—and Newton said it was Hobbs—had no right to do so. If Hobbs's suggestion that he was deceived at the time of the divorce correspondence was worthy of a moment's belief, said Humphreys, Newton deserved "a niche in a cathedral for his generosity" in paying the prisoner huge sums of money for merely writing a few solicitor's letters to Sir Hari Singh.

The jury agreed with these arguments and found Hobbs guilty. Mr. Justice Avory sentenced him to two years imprisonment. But for the fact that he was in a poor state of health and that he had not been brought into the conspiracy until after it had been launched, Hobbs would probably have received a much heavier sentence.

Next day in the House of Commons the Home Secretary, Sir William Joynson-Hicks, was asked to permit trials for blackmail to be held in camera in order that the victims should not be exposed to such terrible publicity as Sir Hari Singh had received and would not in consequence hesitate to go to the police. The Home Secretary replied that he was opposed to secret trials because he feared they would only increase "morbid public curiosity".

At the same time he said he was considering the possibility of making blackmail punishable by flogging as well as by imprisonment. No one seems to have pointed out to him that in the case under discussion the possibility of getting 'the cat' would not have deterred Hobbs, who was in any case much too old and ill to be punished in this way.

9. THE SHOOTING OF P.C. GUTTERIDGE

THE last case with which Sir Travers Humphreys was professionally concerned before his elevation to the Bench was the prosecution of two hardened criminals for the murder of a police constable on a lonely road in Essex. It was a case of peculiar difficulty. The culprits were eventually put in the dock by a brilliant piece of detective work. But the subsequent presentation of the evidence against them by Humphreys as prosecutor required exceptional skill and knowledge of criminal procedure, for the admissibility in court of certain essential portions of this evidence was bound to be severely questioned by the defence.

Police Constable George Gutteridge had been a member of the Essex Constabulary for seventeen years and was stationed at the village of Stapleford Abbots. During the night of September 26, 1927, when he was on duty, he had orders to meet an officer on a neighbouring beat. The meeting took place in the small hours. The conference point was roughly mid-way between Romford and Ongar, which is a quiet rural neighbourhood well away from the main road to London. The two men met and discussed their official business. At about 3 a.m. Gutteridge set off on foot to return home. Just before six o'clock that same morning his body was found a few hundred yards away from the spot where he had met his fellow officer. He had been shot dead.

Two bullets had been fired into his head. Two others had been fired with singular brutality into each eye, apparently while he lay on the ground. Close to his helmet on the ground beside him was his notebook, while his pencil was tightly gripped in his right hand. There were no traces of a struggle, and it seemed as if he was about to take particulars of some person or persons he had met. As his torch was in his pocket and there was no lamp-post anywhere near it looked as if he must have been writing by the light of some vehicle. This impression was confirmed by the mark of a motor tyre at the side of the road. Gutteridge's failure to use his truncheon—as Humphreys explained in opening the case in court—suggested that he had been taken entirely by surprise when the fatal shots were fired at him.

Now it happened that a Morris car had been stolen during the night from the garage of a Dr. Lovell in Billericay, twelve miles away. Next morning the car was found abandoned in Brixton. Bloodstains were noticed on the running-board and an empty cartridge-case was found inside the car, suitable for the size of the bullets which were recovered from Gutteridge's head.

The car was then driven to the scene of the crime, and it was discovered that the tyre exactly fitted the mark on the side of the road. Furthermore, the owner of the car had noted the mileage on the speedometer when he had put it away in the garage on the evening before the murder. The car had travelled forty-three miles although the direct route from Dr. Lovell's house to the place where it was found was only twenty-seven miles. The significance of this was that the thief or thieves had not dared to drive to London by the main route, where police were on patrol, but had travelled by devious by-roads. Experiments carried out by detectives bore out this impression. "In these circumstances," Sir Travers Humphreys told the magistrate at the South-Western Police Court, "you will perhaps agree that if one can find the persons who were the occupants of that motor-car on its run that night from Dr. Lovell's house to Brixton one has gone a long way towards solving the problem of who were the murderers of P.C. Gutteridge."

It had taken a long time to bring the murderers to court. For some weeks the police worked on the case without success. Then about the middle of November something happened to put the police on their trail. A motor-car recklessly driven forced a lorry into a wall in Birmingham and drove on without stopping. The lorry-driver took its number and reported it to the police, who were able to trace it. They then discovered that the particulars of the driving licence as well as the car's number plates were false.

At the same time an informer, doubtless in the hopes of earning the advertised reward, came forward and told the authorities that he had been in the car at the time of the incident with the lorry. He also told them that the driver of the car was a man named Browne who kept a garage in Clapham. And, said the informer, Browne had been concerned with the Gutteridge murder in company with a certain Patrick Kennedy who worked for him in his garage.

Browne—his real name was Leo Brown—was already known to the police as a violent criminal who had operated in Essex. He was forty-six. He specialised in stealing cars. While serving a term of penal servitude in Dartmoor Prison he had met Kennedy, a Clydeside Irishman, ten years his junior.

On their release Browne took Kennedy into his employment as an assistant in his thefts and at the garage where they altered the cars for re-sale. Browne was arrested in Clapham.

Meanwhile Kennedy, who had noticed the police near the garage, had fled to Liverpool with a girl he had lately married. He was discovered in a house behind the Adelphi Hotel and on being challenged by a detective-sergeant he thrust a pistol against the sergeant's ribs and pulled the trigger. He had forgotten to release the safety catch and no harm was done. Kennedy later made a statement to the police in which he admitted being in the car with Browne on the night of the murder, but sought to throw the whole blame on his confederate.

The case for the Crown against Browne and Kennedy was opened by Sir Travers Humphreys before the late Mr. J. B. Sandbach, K.C., the Metropolitan magistrate, on February 13, 1928.

Besides the facts set out by Humphreys these proceedings were interesting because the statements made by the two prisoners to the police were challenged by the defence. When Browne had been cautioned, the inspector had pronounced the customary formula that anything he said might be taken down and used in evidence. Browne's counsel submitted that this was insufficient warning as the words 'against you' had been omitted from the end.

Humphreys replied that under the recent rules approved by His Majesty's judges particular care was now taken to avoid the suggestion that a person's answers could only be used in evidence against him. "It should be known in these days," he added, "that there is no such thing as unfairness on the part of the prosecution." The magistrate thereupon ruled that the statement was admissible.

As for Kennedy's statement, his solicitor objected that it had been obtained by 'third degree' methods after a train journey from Liverpool to London with no sleep and nothing to eat— "pumped out by four hours of interrogation, of promises, hopes and threats." The magistrate said that at the next hearing he would listen to the circumstances in which this statement was taken.

"I was going to suggest the same course," remarked Humphreys. "I will say a few words of explanation when the statement is put in."

He was unable to do so. Before the court sat again Humphreys was raised to the Bench, but he had the satisfaction of seeing it established that no improper methods had been employed by the police to secure Kennedy's statement. This was made clear at the subsequent trial at the Old Bailey, where the statement was accepted by Mr. Justice Avory.

Both men were sentenced to death and executed.

Although Sir Travers Humphreys was not involved in the later stages of this sensational prosecution, he had done all the spadework. Much of the credit must go to him for his part in securing the conviction of two of the most callous and brutal murderers of this century.

10. THE HONEYMOON MYSTERY

PERHAPS the most sensational case which Sir Travers Humphreys had to try during his first year on the Bench was that of a young Chinese named Chun-Yi-Miao, who was accused of murdering his wife while they were on their honeymoon. The trial took place at Carlisle Assizes in 1928. This case depended entirely on circumstantial evidence. It had one unusual feature: the prosecution could offer no explanation of motive. On this Humphreys had some pertinent remarks to make when he came to sum up.

Miao, whose age was twenty-eight, came of a wealthy Chinese family of good standing. He had been a law student in America, and while there had recently married a rich girl named Wai Sheung. This marriage was regarded by the American Press as a romantic affair between two of the best-looking and most attractive members of the younger Chinese set. The couple planned to spend their honeymoon in Europe, and crossed the Atlantic by liner. They went first to Scotland and then to Derwentwater in the Lake District, which they reached on June 18, 1928.

There they attracted considerable attention, partly because they were Chinese and partly because on arrival they began at once to explore the neighbourhood on foot. On the following day they went for a walk on the shores of the lake. In the afternoon Miao returned alone to the hotel. He said he had left his wife, who had gone to Keswick to buy some warm underwear, and that he expected her back to supper. As she had not returned by supper-time he ate the meal alone.

Later he made some casual inquiries about her and suggested a call to the police. Then he went to bed. He was still in bed when the police arrived in the hotel early next morning to arrest him for the murder of his bride. She had been strangled with a double piece of cord near a place about a mile away where her husband had been seen with her the previous afternoon. It seemed that she had first been assaulted. Her left glove had been removed, which at first sight looked as if it was for the purpose of stealing two valuable rings which she had been in the habit of wearing. The rings were subsequently discovered in a spool of film belonging to her husband's camera.

The chain of circumstantial evidence against Miao was strengthened by two further discoveries on the part of the police. The first of these was some cord similar in colour though not in size to that with which she had been strangled. This was found in their hotel room. Inquiries were then made at the hotel where they had stayed in Scotland. The room they occupied there was searched and on the top of a cupboard three pieces of paper were found on which some Chinese characters had been written. Translation revealed these to be three sentences, "Be sure to do it in the ship." "Don't do it in the ship", and "Again consider on arrival in Europe". At the trial it was suggested by the prosecution that Miao had used these pieces of paper to draw lots for some important enterprise—doubtless the murder of his wife. Miao could offer no explanation of the writings.

Briefly the case against him was that he had strangled his wife and had then tried to clear himself by staging the appearance of a brutal murder by a stranger. Miao's defence was based on the assertion that his wife was famous for her jewellery, and had invited robbery by displaying it on all occasions. It was also urged on his behalf that Chinese sailors had been seen in the locality, and had probably followed him and his wife from the boat. Several witnesses indeed gave evidence to this effect.

Furthermore, as Miao's counsel suggested, "the string was tied in a 'granny knot'—the sort of knot that sailors use." "I hope sailors don't," remarked Mr. Justice Humphreys, himself a keen yachtsman.

As for the missing rings which had been found in the camera spool, the prisoner said that his wife must have put them there before going out for her last walk in order to save herself the trouble of locking them in her jewel case.

In his summing-up Humphreys could not disguise the fact that the weight of the evidence was against the prisoner, although he was careful to bring out all the points there were in his favour. For example, Humphreys pointed out it was remarkable that nobody had seen the girl in Keswick, where Miao swore she had gone, though every other journey made by the couple or either of them in the short period of their stay in Cumberland had been observed by several other people.

Against this the judge set Miao's explanation that she had probably been prevented from going to Keswick at all. Then there was the fact that Madame Miao, a stranger to the district, should have decided to make a journey of several miles without knowing what means of transport existed. On the other hand, her husband had testified that she spoke of hiring a car. Finally there was Miao's odd behaviour in going to bed after making only general observations on his wife's absence. On this point Humphreys recalled the prosecution's argument that "bridegrooms do not usually exhibit such stolidity".

Humphreys then put the matter in a nutshell to the jury. "Do you accept his explanation that there was a misunderstanding on the part of a number of persons?" he asked them. "Or do you take the view that he is a man who has committed a foul murder, who was clever enough to feign emotion and clever enough to try and cover up his tracks, and who has given plausible, but not acceptable, explanations of his evidence?"

The jury accepted the latter alternative and found Miao guilty. He appealed to the Court of Criminal Appeal, where he delivered a long speech in fluent English, but his appeal was dismissed. The Home Secretary refused to intervene and he was duly hanged.

The question remains, why did Miao murder his wife? No convincing reason was suggested at the trial. However, as Mr. Justice Humphreys commented there, it is not necessary for the prosecution to establish the motive for any crime. "There is always some reason why a crime is committed except in cases of insanity," he told the jury, "but it sometimes happens that the prosecution is unable to call any evidence as to that reason."

It was subsequently suggested that Miao was not so financially

MRS. ELVIRA BARNEY

well off as he claimed to be, and that his wife, as a modern woman, might have refused to conform to the ancient Chinese customs in regard to a married woman's property. It has also been suggested that Miao was the agent of a Chinese 'Tong' secret society which desired to kill his wife out of revenge against her family or for financial benefit. Nevertheless, the crime remains a mystery. One thing, however, is firmly established. There has never been any suggestion based on any sort of reasonable ground that Miao was unjustly convicted and executed.

11. THE TRIAL OF MRS. BARNEY

AMONG the many murder trials, at which Sir Travers Humphreys has presided, that of Mrs. Elvira Dolores Barney stands out. She was a Mayfair society beauty who was accused of killing her lover in 1932. Both Mrs. Barney and the victim in this case belonged to the gay set which gallivanted round London between the two world wars, and whose members were known as the Bright Young People. They drank far more than was good for them, tore about the town in bright-coloured sports cars, and even brighter-coloured clothes, played absurd and sometimes unkind practical jokes, indulged in riotous parties, as well as promiscuous sexual intercourse, and generally made nuisances of themselves.

At the time of the tragic happening, which brought her to the dock in the Old Bailey, Mrs. Barney was living apart from her husband in a mews flat off Knightsbridge, near Hyde Park. She was twenty-six, had blonde, fluffy hair, plenty of money and a taste for dissipation. Her parents were titled people with a house in Belgrave Square and a country seat in Sussex.

Her lover, Michael Stephen, was a year younger than Mrs. Barney. He, also, came of a good family, but having early developed wild and extravagant habits had been turned out of the house by his father, and now occupied a bed-sitting-room in the Brompton Road. He had described himself as a dress designer, but he had no regular occupation, unless it was

F

sponging on women. He had known Mrs. Barney for about a year, and during this period had been quite content to be kept by his new mistress. At times they would make love with fierce abandonment; at other times their relations would be marked by stormy scenes, when they would quarrel far into the night.

One evening in May, Mrs. Barney gave a cocktail party, at which some twenty-five people were present at various times. Stephen busied himself handing round the drinks. After the guests had left he and Mrs. Barney had dined at the Café de Paris. They went on to a Soho night-club, the Blue Angel, where they stayed till about 1 a.m. Mrs. Barney paid the bills. They returned to her flat, where they proceeded to have one of their quarrels, apparently over another woman whom Stephen was fond of. Some time after three o'clock shouts were heard coming from the flat, followed by a shot.

A few minutes later Mrs. Barney telephoned frantically for a doctor. "There has been a terrible accident," she screamed. "For God's sake come at once."

When the doctor arrived he found Stephen lying fully dressed at the top of the stairs with a bullet through his lung. He was already dead. Near him lay a pistol, containing five cartridges, of which two were spent. "He can't be dead," sobbed Mrs. Barney. "I will die, too. I want to die. I loved him so."

Soon afterwards the police arrived and began to make investigations, from which it was clear that the dead man could not possibly have taken his own life. As the experts were later to testify in court, there had been a struggle, in the course of which his finger could not have been on the trigger of the revolver.

Three days later Mrs. Barney was arrested in her parents' house in Belgrave Square and charged with murder.

The trial took place at the Central Criminal Court on July 4, 1932, and the two succeeding days. Mrs. Barney was defended by Sir Patrick Hastings, while the prosecution was conducted by Mr. Percival Clarke. Mr. Justice Humphreys was on the Bench.

The principal Crown witness on the first day was the wife of one of the chauffeurs who lived in the mews. In her original statement to the police she had stated that just before the fatal shot was fired she had heard Mrs. Barney say, "Get out, I'll shoot you." This had been repeated by Clarke in his opening speech. But in the witness-box she changed the words to, "Get out. I'll shoot," a vital difference with which Sir Patrick made great play later when he came to address the jury.

Mrs. Barney's counsel did not touch on this point in his cross-examination of this witness, for fear she might go back on her statement. He preferred instead to concentrate on an earlier incident which occurred three weeks before, when Mrs. Barney had fired the revolver near the window and then looked out. Afterwards the witness had spoken to Stephen. What was their conversation?

Prosecuting counsel immediately objected that what the witness had said to the young man outside Mrs. Barney's hearing was not admissible as evidence. But after hearing Hastings argue that it was always admissible to give evidence of a statement accompanying such an incident Mr. Justice Humphreys allowed it and directed the cross-examination to proceed.

"What conversation passed between you and the young man?" asked Hastings.

"I told him to clear off, as he was a perfect nuisance in the mews," replied the chauffeur's wife.

"What did he reply?"

"He said he didn't want to leave Mrs. Barney because *he was afraid that she might kill herself.*"

This was an admission of cardinal importance for the defence, since it corroborated Mrs. Barney's own story, when she went into the witness-box, that she had fired the revolver on the previous occasion with the intention of making Stephen think she was going to commit suicide. The cause of their quarrel on that occasion, she said, was her refusal to finance his gambling. "When he was outside," she went on, "I fired the pistol at random in the room. Then I thought, if he really believed I had killed myself, he'd go and fetch people, so I looked out of the window."

As for what happened on the fatal night, Mrs. Barney's story was that she had threatened, as she had done before, to shoot herself if her lover went away with another woman. Stephen's reply had been, "Well, you won't do it with this," picking up the revolver. She struggled to get hold of it and so the shot was fired. In short, it was an accident. That was the story she had also told the doctor and the police.

"What right have we to say that the story is untrue?" Mr. Justice Humphreys asked the jury in his summing-up. According to the doctor she was very hysterical and over-wrought at the time, a factor which tended to preclude the invention of a cool and connected fabrication. Unless the jury rejected this story completely, the judge warned them, they would have difficulty in finding her guilty of murder.

On the other hand, there was the question of manslaughter. "Manslaughter," he directed the jury, "is the *unlawful* killing of another without any *intention* of either killing or causing serious injury."

The judge then proceeded to apply this definition to the case before them. "It amounts to this," he said, "if the prisoner threatened to commit suicide—suicide, let me remind you, is a crime—and the deceased man removed the revolver in order to prevent it, and she, in order to carry out her intention, struggled with him and so caused the revolver to go off, she would then be guilty of manslaughter and so answerable for that offence at law."

This passage in the judge's summing-up corresponded exactly to Mrs. Barney's account of what had taken place. Nevertheless, the jury, undoubtedly influenced by Hastings's impassioned defence—the judge said his concluding speech was one of the finest he had ever heard delivered at the Bar—brought in a verdict of not guilty, either of manslaughter or murder.

Contrary to his usual custom Mr. Justice Humphreys did not comment on this verdict when it was delivered.

44

12. THE FIRE RAISERS

WE are all familiar with the detective story of fiction in which the authorities are enabled to track down the criminal through the aid of an outside investigator. Such a story does not often happen in real life. Yet it did happen in the case of Leopold Harris and his gang of fire raisers who were tried by Sir Travers Humphreys in 1933. It was an amazing case, in which a London solicitor, by much perseverance and a certain amount of good luck, brought off what must surely be the most sensational feat of private detection in history.

As a result Harris and sixteen other prisoners, including a woman, eventually stood in the dock at the Old Bailey charged with defrauding insurance companies by presenting bogus claims. Their trial lasted for thirty-three days and was the longest, and probably the most complex, which has ever been heard there. Apart from the accused, three men whose names were mentioned in the evidence anticipated their arrest by committing suicide. One poisoned himself with disinfectant, another was found asphyxiated in his garage, while the third threw himself in front of an Underground railway train, after first carefully removing his gold wrist-watch and placing it on the platform.

Harris described himself as an insurance assessor, but it would be more accurate to call him a 'claims-maker', since his function was invariably to represent the victim of a burglary or fire and to prepare the appropriate claim against the insurance company concerned. He operated an intelligence service which kept him posted of fires and burglaries throughout the country. On receiving news of one he would be quickly on the scene, and would offer to prepare the claim on behalf of the insured for a five per cent commission. His claims were always greatly inflated, and he was in consequence much distrusted by the insurance companies. Among those with whom he frequently crossed swords over claims was Mr. William Charles Crocker, a solicitor who specialised in insurance work.

The prosecution of Harris and his confederates was conducted by Mr. Roland Oliver, K.C., now Mr. Justice Oliver, and the tale of the prisoner's misdeeds which he related in court made both judge and jury gasp by reason of their bare-faced effrontery.

Briefly, what happened was this. Harris got tired of present-ing claims mainly for the benefit of others, and he decided to use more direct and lucrative methods of swindling insurance companies. His plan, which he carried out on an extensive scale, was to float dummy businesses, put them in the name of a confederate as owner, insure them for fantastic sums in respect of fire loss and 'loss of profits', and having burnt them down and thus destroyed the stock, present huge claims, ostensibly on behalf of his clients but actually on behalf of himself and his fellow conspirators. For this purpose he enlisted two members of his family, his brother David and his brother-in-law Harry Gould (formerly Goldstein), a tailor, who had developed an interest in fires as a buyer of salvaged goods. Gould's firm was the main source from which Harris obtained 'stock' for his warehouses. The two other chief con-spirators were Louis Jarvis (formerly Jacobs) and Camillo Capsoni, an Italian who had been in the silk trade.

The first big fire mentioned in the trial occurred in 1927, when the warehouse of Fabrique de Soieries Ltd. went up in flames at Manchester. Jarvis and Capsoni were its nominal proprietors, but in reality Harris had a substantial share in it. Its stock, which consisted of depreciated Italian silk from Gould's firm, was insured for £40,000, though its actual value was only a tenth of that figure. There was also a 'loss of profits' policy with Lloyd's for £20,000. Harris, who had con-veniently arranged to be in Manchester on the night of the fire, proceeded to handle the claims, which were eventually settled by the insurers for £29,000.

Thereafter Harris adopted similar methods all over the country, not stopping at bribery to serve his ends. The insurance companies naturally employed their own independent assessors to examine and adjust the claims, but Harris's know-ledge of the individual assessors usually retained by each fire office was such that he deliberately placed insurance where he knew that the assessors likely to be sent to investigate claims possessed personal weaknesses of which he could take advantage for his own ends. On the other hand, Crocker, the solicitor, continually contested Harris's grossly exaggerated claims, and in a certain instance was able to effect very substantial reductions, but as yet he had no evidence of fraud.

Then Mr. Crocker had two pieces of luck. First, a man named Mathews, who had been a clerk in Lloyd's and consequently knew of the solicitor's connection with the insurance world, came to him with an amazing story. According to Mathews, a friend of his had been approached by a certain Harry Priest, who told him that a mysterious personage, whom Priest referred to as 'The Prince', would set him up in a bogus business, which in due course was to be burnt down, so that everyone could benefit at the expense of the insurance companies. Crocker's reaction was to tell Mathews to ask his friend to keep in touch with Priest and find out more about 'The Prince', who was, of course, none other than Leopold Harris himself.

A little later Mathews returned with the exciting news that Priest had told him that a 'bric-à-brac' shop in Poland Street, off Oxford Street, was being fitted out by 'The Prince' and would shortly go up in flames. Sure enough, in a week or two this is exactly what happened.

With the backing of Lloyd's and one of the principal fire offices, Crocker decided to concentrate on investigating this and similar losses. He found that Priest was a partner in a silk business at Stoke Newington. He then managed to obtain a photograph of him leaving the warehouse, on the pretext of collecting evidence of a motor accident. Crocker also discovered that Priest's partner was the Italian Capsoni, who had recently had a fire in another business with which he was associated, the Franco-Italian Silk Company in Oxford Street. Capsoni also turned out to be the source from which the owner of the bric-à-brac shop in Poland Street had acquired £1,400 worth of Venetian glass, which had figured in the insurance claim after the fire there.

Crocker's next stroke of luck was when Capsoni's Scottish

wife walked into his office one day not long afterwards. She had been sent by Captain Miles, the head of the London Salvage Corps, an official body subsidised by the fire insurance companies to protect their interests and co-operate with the Metropolitan fire brigades in saving life and property at fires. Miles was one of the select few who had been let into the secret of Crocker's investigations. It appeared that Mrs. Capsoni had in turn been sent to Miles by an insurance official whom she had told that she had seen a photograph of Harris's confidante, Louis Jarvis, as being concerned with a fire at Wembley, and that she had reason to believe that Jarvis had committed arson.

Mrs. Capsoni now made a complete confession. She told Crocker that she and her husband had belonged to the Harris gang, but had lately been troubled with conscientious scruples and they now wished to return to an honest way of life. She then went out and fetched Capsoni, who confirmed her account of how he had set fire to the Manchester warehouse of Fabrique de Soieries in 1927. There is no doubt that the Capsonis' repentance was genuine, but of course as erstwhile accomplices their evidence would require independent corroboration if the jury was to be convinced of the gang's guilt.

In an attempt to obtain further evidence directly implicating Harris, Crocker faked a motor accident to Capsoni, who agreed to say that this was engineered by the gang to 'bump him off', and his wife would warn Harris that he intended to go to Scotland Yard, when he had recovered, unless Harris visited him with an assurance that he was not behind the accident. Concealed microphones at the bedside would record Harris's conversation. Everything went according to plan, except that Harris flatly refused to visit the hospital. Someone or something had occurred to arouse his suspicions.

However, Crocker, who had by this time been instructed by the Director of Public Prosecutions to act as his agent, was able by following up the files of the insurance companies and other clues to establish the complicity of Harris and his gang in no less than twenty fires. The evidence was considered sufficient to justify the arrest of the fire raisers. While they were in custody 26,000 Bank of England notes were traced through their numbers as having passed through the hands of Harris and his agents.

The final scene in the Old Bailey was probably unique. Roland Oliver's brief for the prosecution was two feet high, a room in the court building had to be specially set aside for the accommodation of the documents in the case, and Mr. Justice Humphreys gave permission for a so-called 'whispering telephone' to be put beside Crocker in court. In reality it was an ordinary Post Office instrument with specially powerful batteries and a tuned-up microphone, which Crocker could use to communicate with the outside world without disturbing the proceedings in court. It was in fact used at the judge's suggestion to recall a witness who had gone to his house at Bognor and was eventually found swimming in the sea.

Mr. Justice Humphreys's summing-up lasted for thirteen hours, the longest ever delivered at the Old Bailey. The jury then found all the prisoners guilty. Harris as the ringleader got fourteen years penal servitude and the others were sentenced to lesser terms. They included Priest, who was defended by the judge's son Christmas Humphreys.

It later transpired that Captain Miles of the London Salvage Corps was also in Harris's pay and that it was he who had warned his master not to go and see Capsoni in hospital. He was tried later in the year and went to prison for four years.

All the barristers instructed in the fire-raising case presented Mr. Justice Humphreys with a silver ink-stand when it was over. The judge in turn excused the jury from any further jury service for the rest of their lives, unless, as he added with a smile, "any one of you has a yearning to perform it again".

13. THE DOUBLE CONFESSION MURDER

ONE of the strangest cases which Mr. Justice Humphreys had to try—a case which earned him considerable praise when it was later reviewed in the Court of Criminal Appeal—was the trial of Mrs. Alma Rattenbury and George Stoner for the murder of Mrs. Rattenbury's husband in 1935.

The dead man, Francis Rattenbury, was a retired architect, aged sixty-seven, who lived in Bournemouth. His wife, a Canadian by birth and a musician of considerable talent, was thirty-eight. Each had been previously married. Stoner, their chauffeur and odd-job man, who was jointly charged with her, was a youth of eighteen.

Rattenbury was found in his house in Bournemouth suffering from severe head injuries, from which he soon died. Mrs. Rattenbury confessed to the police that she had killed her husband in a fit of temper and she was thereupon arrested. A day or two later the police also arrested Stoner as he was sitting in the Rattenburys' car outside the house. On being cautioned, he said that he alone had committed the crime and that Mrs. Rattenbury knew nothing about it. "I did the job," he said. "I believe he was asleep. I hit him and then went upstairs and told Mrs. Rattenbury."

The police were thus faced with two suspects, each of whom claimed to have done the murder and each of whom exonerated the other. Each had both opportunity and motive.

The Rattenburys had been married for seven years and, though quarrels were not uncommon, they had lived fairly comfortably together. However, it was soon discovered that Stoner, who lived in the house with his employers, was on terms of considerable intimacy with Mrs. Rattenbury. In fact, she was his mistress in more senses than one. But in this, according to her own story in court, she was not obstructed in any way by her husband, who had told her to "live her own life".

Only a few days before the attack on Rattenbury, Stoner and Mrs. Rattenbury had spent a night together secretly in London, one object of this trip apparently being to buy clothes for Stoner. They appeared to be very much in love with each other.

It was the maid in the house who gave the alarm by sending for the doctor when she saw Mrs. Rattenbury screaming with hysteria and obviously drunk. When he arrived the doctor gave Mrs. Rattenbury some morphia to quieten her and sent her to bed. But shortly afterwards she came down and told the police, who had now taken charge, that she suspected her husband's son by his previous marriage to have murdered him. On being taken to the police station, Mrs. Rattenbury told the inspector that she would let him know in the morning "where the mallet was", thus implying that it was she who had attacked her husband. But later she signed a statement to the effect that she had been playing cards with him on the previous evening and that he had dared her to kill him. She had then hit him with a mallet. "I'd have shot him if I'd had a gun," she added. However, on being committed for trial she withdrew this statement and pleaded not guilty.

At the trial Mr. Justice Humphreys made it clear to the jury that Mrs. Rattenbury's admissions had been made when she was under the influence of alcohol and morphia. The maid testified that she was incapable of holding a saucer properly when she brought her a cup of coffee. By the time the police came on the scene, said the maid, Mrs. Rattenbury was practically raving and tried to kiss them.

The judge then questioned the maid closely as to whether her mistress had been in the habit of taking drugs, "things like cocaine, morphia or heroin", but this was denied both by the maid and Mrs. Rattenbury herself when she went into the witness-box to tell her own story. Nevertheless, in view of this evidence about her condition the judge directed that the jury should be shown specimens of her handwriting in her cheque-books to compare with that of her statement given to the police.

The wretched Stoner had also withdrawn his confession and pleaded not guilty at the trial. His counsel subsequently suggested to the jury that the proper verdict in his case should be 'guilty but insane'. But Mr. Justice Humphreys at once told the jury that they should judge the case on the evidence and should disregard this half-admission of guilt by Stoner's counsel.

Stoner did not go into the box and give evidence. But two doctors were called on his behalf. One stated that his appearance was consistent with his being addicted to cocaine. The other doctor expressed the opinion that jealousy often resulted from the cocaine habit.

Stoner's counsel submitted that his client's assault upon the dead man was like the impulsive act of a child and that his mind was incapable of forming the necessary 'intent' which would make the crime one of murder.

In his summing-up Mr. Justice Humphreys told the jury that, in spite of what the two doctors had said, in his view there was no evidence to support the suggestion that at the time of the fatal blow Stoner was under the influence of drugs and did not know what he was doing. Since he had been in prison, added the judge, Stoner had given no reason for supposing that he was other than a perfectly healthy person, nor had he shown any signs which commonly follow the sudden cessation of cocaine-taking. "It is a pitiable thing that he, at the age of eighteen, should have been brought to this pass," Mr. Justice Humphreys went on, "and I do not think I am putting it too unfairly, even against Mrs. Rattenbury, when I say that, whatever your verdict may be, his position is due to the domination of this woman."

The judge then set out the law relating to persons charged with this kind of crime. He explained that it was unnecessary, in order to establish their guilt, that a person aiding and abetting the crime should be present at the moment the deed was actually committed. Nor did it matter whose hand struck the fatal blow, if both agreed that it should be struck. At the same time, he pointed out, both the accused had separately affirmed and denied their part in the killing of Rattenbury. "It may be," said the judge, referring to the female prisoner, "that you will say that you cannot possibly feel any sympathy for this woman, that you cannot have any feeling except of disgust for her. But beware that you do not convict her of this crime with which she is charged because she is an adulteress—and an adulteress, you may think, of the most unpleasant type."

The jury of ten men and two women were absent from the court room for less than an hour. When they returned, it was to bring in a verdict of not guilty against Mrs. Rattenbury and guilty against Stoner. In the case of Stoner they added a recommendation to mercy. The judge then assumed the black cap, as he was bound to do, and sentenced Stoner to death.

But the case did not end there. On her discharge Mrs. Rattenbury was taken to a nursing home. Two days later she left, against the matron's wish, in order, she said, to organise the campaign for Stoner's reprieve. Next day her body was found floating in the River Stour, near Bournemouth, with apparently self-inflicted wounds. She left several letters behind, in which she stated her desire to kill herself because of Stoner's conviction. At the inquest the coroner's jury recorded a verdict of suicide while temporarily insane.

A week afterwards Stoner lodged an appeal. At the same time a petition for his reprieve, signed by more than 300,000 people, was presented to the Home Secretary by Bournemouth's M.P.s. There were three grounds for the appeal. First, that the two should have been tried separately; second, that Stoner should now be called as a witness, seeing that the death of Mrs. Rattenbury had freed him from the necessity of preserving a chivalrous silence; and thirdly that the judge had slurred over the evidence which indicated that Stoner might be a drug addict.

The appeal was dismissed, but in view of the prisoner's youth the Home Secretary immediately commuted the sentence to one of penal servitude for life.

II. LORD SIMON AND HIS CASES

LORD SIMON

II. LORD SIMON AND HIS CASES

1. LORD SIMON

FOR many years before his death, early in 1954, Lord Simon stood without challenge as the greatest lawyer in the country, possibly in the English-speaking world. The range of his knowledge and learning was immense. His memory was prodigious.

Not long before he died he spoke to me for more than an hour, without a note, on some of his experiences in the courts and in Parliament. He paused only once in his discourse, and that was to check the exact wording of a statement he had made in the House of Commons forty years previously.

It was the same with his performance in the House of Lords and the Judicial Committee of the Privy Council. There his judgments are invariably a mixture of polished urbanity and erudition.

In 1952 he presided over a most complicated appeal to the Privy Council involving the ownership of a fleet of airplanes in Hongkong which were claimed by the Chinese People's Government as their property. Not only did Lord Simon's personality dominate the whole proceedings, but he conveyed the impression of knowing more about the subject of the lawsuit that anyone else living.

On the legislative side of the House of Lords he remained active until within a few weeks of his death. He spoke on his negotiations with Egypt just before Parliament rose for the Christmas recess in December, 1953, and on the previous day he initiated a debate on capital punishment.

For thirty-nine years he was a Member of Parliament, nineteen of them as Minister. For fourteen years before his death he was a Law Lord. Yet there was none of the pomposity about him which people sometimes expect from legal pundits and elder statesmen. He was straightforward and direct of speech.

57   G

Lord Simon once remarked that there are two things needed for success at the English Bar. The first is a good clerk and the second is a good digestion. He had both, and the combination enabled him to work hour after hour at a pressure under which most other men would have broken down.

To a considerable extent he modelled his style of advocacy on that of the late Lord Carson, who believed in getting straight to the point of a case without any frills. Like Carson, too, Lord Simon realised at the outset of his legal career that in cross-examining a witness in court the first question is of supreme importance. It must go to the root of the matter which the barrister wishes to establish, whether this happens to be a question of fact or is merely designed to show the unreliability of the man or woman giving evidence in the witness-box.

It was Carson who, in the year 1903, got Simon his first big brief at the Bar. Carson was Solicitor-General and suddenly found himself obliged at short notice to conduct an extremely difficult case on behalf of the British Government with the United States of America. The subject of dispute was the boundary between Canada and the American territory of Alaska. There were thousands of documents involved, including old maps, treaties and memoranda, many in French and Russian. Carson, who hated any case with bulky correspondence and anyhow had little or no knowledge of foreign languages, was in despair until he suddenly remembered that a young man not long down from Oxford named John Simon had written an opinion for him on another matter of international law. He asked Mr. Simon to help; Simon willingly agreed.

The case eventually went to arbitration and Mr. Simon was instructed to appear in it with the Solicitor-General. It was a tremendous stroke of luck, since the dispute was bound to be long, expensive and of historical importance. As it turned out, the young junior counsel (he was barely thirty) rendered the greatest assistance in the case and attracted much attention to himself through his industry and knowledge.

From that moment Simon prospered. He entered the House

of Commons in 1906 as Liberal member for Walthamstow.
Two years later he put on the silk gown of a K.C. In 1911 at
the age of thirty-seven he became the youngest Solicitor-
General in modern times. Two years afterwards he was
promoted to be Attorney-General. Then, on the formation of
the First Coalition Government by Mr. Asquith in 1915, the
Prime Minister offered him the Woolsack. But the prospect of
leaving the House of Commons and becoming Lord Chancellor
at the age of forty-two did not appeal to him and he turned it
down. Instead he went to the Home Office, a job which left
him free to return to the Bar when he wished. Twenty-five
years later Asquith's offer was repeated by Sir Winston (then
Mr.) Churchill. This time he accepted it.

John Allsebrook Simon, later Viscount Simon, was born in
Manchester, where his father was a Congregational minister.
The impression has persisted that he was of Jewish origin.
This is not so. For many years he did not trouble to correct
it, believing as he did that his denial might be distorted by
malicious gossip into some sympathy with anti-Semitism—
"an attitude," to quote his own words, "which I regard as
un-English and which I heartily condemn". He eventually did
so after he became Foreign Secretary in 1931, when it was
represented to him that the false rumour as to his antecedents
was injurious to British policy abroad. His father's people had
come from Pembrokeshire and the name Simon, like other
Biblical names, is quite common in that part of Wales.

John Simon grew up as a youthful prodigy. He went to a
Scottish public school, Fettes College, where he won the top
entrance scholarship and carried off all the school prizes, ending
up as head boy. He gained equal distinctions at Wadham
College, Oxford, and later at All Souls, of which college he
became the Senior Fellow. In his first year as a barrister he
made twenty-seven guineas. But his practice grew rapidly. By
the time he left the Temple for good, thirty-one years later, he
was said to be earning more than £30,000 a year. He took
seemingly infinite pains over the preparation of his cases. Yet
to the onlooker his performances in court appeared ridicu-
lously easy and effortless. As an envious rival remarked, "It's

as though you put a penny in the slot at one end and the verdict pops out at the other".

In politics Lord Simon was less happy. For joining Mr. Ramsay MacDonald's National Government he was bitterly assailed as a turncoat by his former Liberal colleagues. It was of him that Lloyd George remarked that "the right hon. gentleman has sat so long upon the fence that the iron has entered into his soul". His tenure of the Foreign Office was associated with the disastrous policy of appeasement. But it should be remembered that this policy commanded the support of the leaders of all the political parties in England at the time. He was, however, an excellent Home Secretary, first in 1915 and again twenty years later. Probably his most effective political intervention took place during the General Strike in 1926, when an outspoken speech which he delivered had much to do with the ending of the stoppage.

Lord Simon was at heart a friendly man, though he himself would probably admit that he lacked what is known as 'the common touch'. Few of his many acquaintances and friends called him by his first name: he gave the impression that he was desperately anxious that they should do so. Possibly his tendency to aloofness and reserve became ingrained after the death of his first wife during his early years at the Bar, and a long time was to elapse before he again found domestic concord in a happy second marriage.

In 1952 he published a volume of memoirs, but he has had little to say in them about his experience at the Bar. Perhaps this is because the advocate is inclined to lose interest in a case the moment it is finished. Yet Lord Simon was briefed in many celebrated trials, some of which are described in the following pages. They include the first German Spy trial in the 1914–18 War, the Russell Divorce case, the Mr. 'A' case, the Bath Club case, the Portuguese banknote swindle, the prosecution of the financiers Hooley and Bottomley for fraud, and numerous other cases of interest and importance.

For a long while Simon was pre-eminent in the courts. If he had not the power to sway juries like some advocates, none could present a case more logically and more lucidly. For

sheer intellectual superiority in the law he had no equal in his
time.

2. THE MAN WHO LIBELLED KING GEORGE V

A FEW months after King George V ascended the Throne in
1910, Sir John Simon, as Lord Simon then was, became His
Majesty's Solicitor-General at the age of thirty-seven. One of
his first duties as a Law Officer was to assist in the prosecution of a remarkable, and indeed unprecedented, Crown case,
which personally concerned the wearer of the Crown. The
prisoner in the case was charged with publishing a foul and
malicious libel about the King's private life.

The libel was contained in a journal called *The Liberator*,
which was printed in Paris. This journal, in reality little more
than a scandal sheet, was devoted to the dissemination of
Republican propaganda, under the direction of its American
editor, Edward Holden James. Copies were distributed in
England by his agent, a young man of Republican sympathies
named Mylius, who had also supplied the information on
which the libel was based.

The libel took the form of an article, which appeared under
the heading 'Sanctified Bigamy'. It began by stating that during
the year 1890, in the island of Malta, the King had contracted
a lawful marriage with the daughter of a British Admiral, Sir
Michael Culme-Seymour, and that offspring had been born of
this marriage. Having pointed out that at the time of this
marriage the Duke of Clarence, who subsequently died, was
heir to the Throne, the article continued:

"It is now that we are offered the spectacle of the immorality
of the Monarchy in all its sickening, beastly monstrosity. In
order to obtain the woman of Royal blood for his pretended
wife, George Frederick foully abandoned his true wife, the
daughter of Sir Michael Culme-Seymour, of the British Navy,
and entered into a sham and shameful marriage with the
daughter of the Duke of Teck in 1893."

The article went on to charge the King with having committed the crime of bigamy, with the aid and complicity of prelates of the Anglican Church. In conclusion, it asserted that the Admiral's daughter, if she were still alive, was the rightful Queen of England and that her children were the only rightful heirs to the English Throne.

The suggestion was that, having become heir to the Throne, the King put aside the wife whom he had married in 1890 in order to enter into an alliance with a Princess which would be valid by virtue of the Royal Marriage Act. A more cruel and horrible libel it would be difficult to imagine.

It was open to the prosecution to charge Mylius with publishing a seditious libel. In this event the prisoner would have been unable to plead, as he did at the outset of the present case, that what had been written was in fact true, since under our law an attack on the Sovereign is a crime whether there is reason in the attack or not. However, the King had no wish to take advantage of his privileged position, so it was decided to proceed in the ordinary way, just as any of his subjects might do who had been criminally libelled.

There was one constitutional difficulty. The King was willing and anxious to give evidence on oath refuting the libellous allegations. He could, for instance, prove quite easily that he had never been in Malta in 1890 or indeed at any time when the Culme-Seymour family were there. But all the Solicitor-General's researches were unable to produce any instance where the Sovereign had been allowed to go into the witness-box. In order to establish his case the King was consequently obliged to rely on other witnesses.

The trial of Edward Frederick Mylius, accused of criminally libelling King George V, took place before the Lord Chief Justice, Lord Alverstone, and a jury on February 1, 1911. With Sir John Simon, for the prosecution, also appeared Sir Rufus Isaacs, later Lord Reading, the Attorney-General, and Mr. Sidney Rowlatt, later Mr. Justice Rowlatt. The prisoner was not professionally represented, although it was clear that his opening statement, with which he considerably startled the court, had not been framed without legal assistance.

At the solicitors' table, in front of the Crown counsel, sat the Liberal Home Secretary, Mr. Winston Churchill, M.P., who had an official interest in the trial. Mrs. Churchill, also an interested spectator, was accommodated with a seat in the judge's private gallery.

Before the jury were sworn, the prisoner made a remarkable request. "I wish to ask if the King is present," he said. Asked by the judge to repeat what he had said, the young man in the dock proceeded to elaborate it. "I demand his presence," he declared, "on the grounds, first, that every accused person has the right to be confronted with his accuser in court; secondly, that no action for libel is usually taken without the prosecutor being in court, where the jury can see him; and thirdly, that there is no proof that the prosecutor is at present alive."

As it happened, Mylius had already attempted unsuccessfully to have a subpœna served on the King to attend the trial and give evidence. The Lord Chief Justice addressed him sternly. "You are perfectly well aware that the King cannot be summoned here. The King is not present." The judge thereupon ruled that the trial should proceed.

The first witness for the prosecution was a detective, who proved that he had seen Mylius post copies of *The Liberator* with the defamatory article from Notting Hill post office.

Sir John Simon then called Admiral Culme-Seymour. The Admiral said he had had two daughters. Elizabeth, the elder, was married and was now Mrs. Napier; Laura, the younger, was dead. The first time they visited Malta was in 1893, when he was Commander-in-Chief of the Mediterranean Fleet. He swore the King was never in Malta at any time when he and his daughters were there. Indeed, Laura had never spoken to the King in her life and had only seen him once at a garden party in London. The married daughter had only spoken to him once, and Mrs. Napier herself confirmed this in her evidence.

The next witness was the Crown Advocate in Malta, who had charge of all marriage registers in the island. He pointed out that under Maltese law registration of marriages was compulsory. He went on to say that he had personally searched the registers for the period between 1886 and 1893.

"Will you tell us," Sir John Simon asked him, "whether in all those registers, through that series of years, there is any entry of a lady bearing the name of Seymour, or Culme, or Culme-Seymour?"

"There is not," answered the witness.

"Is there any entry in those registers which gives the slightest suspicion or support to what is here suggested?"

"Not the slightest."

The prisoner declined to cross-examine any of the Crown witnesses. Nor did he make any pretence to substantiate the truth of the libel, although he had previously declared he was ready to prove it. Finally, he tried to call the King as his own witness and, on being told that this was constitutionally impossible, he put up no further defence.

Without leaving the court the jury found Mylius guilty. He was immediately sentenced to twelve months imprisonment, the judge remarking that it was unnecessary to pass a heavier sentence.

A document, which lay on the bench beside the Solicitor-General, was then read out. It was signed by the King's own hand and stated categorically that he had never been married except to Queen Mary and that he had never gone through any ceremony of marriage except with the Queen. The King added that he would have attended the trial in person to give evidence to this effect had not the Law Officers advised him that such an act would be unconstitutional.

Thus was the King's honour publicly vindicated and a libel on the name of the Sovereign proved false.

3. The 'Titanic' Disaster

A TRAGEDY which shook the world and is still an abiding memory was the dramatic sinking of the ocean-going liner *Titanic* on her maiden voyage in the North Atlantic over forty years ago. The ship, which struck an iceberg, went down with a loss of nearly 1,500 lives. In the official inquiry into the disaster which followed, Lord Simon, who as Sir John Simon was then Solicitor-General, appeared along with the Attorney-General, Sir Rufus Isaacs, later Lord Reading, for the Board of Trade, which is the Government department responsible for framing the regulations for the safety of merchant vessels.

The *Titanic* was a three-screw vessel of some 46,000 gross tons. She had been built by Messrs. Harland and Wolff in their Belfast yards for the White Star Line. She was the largest ship ever to have come off the slipways till then, and she had been designed not so much to compete with other vessels in speed as to surpass them in luxury and also in safety. She had every amenity conceivable in those days, including magnificently appointed lounges and dining-rooms, shops and a gymnasium. She had water-tight doors, which could be closed in half a minute from the bridge, automatic fire-alarms, the most powerful wireless installations afloat, double bottoms and fifteen water-tight compartments, of which any two could be smashed without endangering the safety of the ship. Indeed she was supposed to be unsinkable.

She set sail from Southampton for New York on April 10, 1912. The course she followed, after making brief calls at Cherbourg and Queenstown, was the accepted route for mail steamers, known as the 'outward southern track'. This roughly described the arc of a circle between the Fastnet Light, off the south-west coast of Ireland, and the Nantucket Lightship, off Long Island Sound. In addition to a crew of 900, she carried more than 1,300 passengers—over 2,200 souls in all. The passenger list contained many distinguished names and included Mr. Bruce Ismay, managing director of the White Star Line; W. T. Stead, the famous Radical journalist; Benjamin Guggenheim, the financier; Sir Cosmo Duff-Gordon, Bart. and many others. Besides the 325 first-class and 285 second-class passengers, there were over 700 third-class passengers. Many of the latter were emigrants and carried with them their small stock of personal possessions to the new world in which they hoped to start life anew beyond the Atlantic. Barely a third was destined to do so.

All went well for four days. The weather was clear and the sea calm, and everyone on board was pleased to be participating in such an auspicious maiden trip. Half-way across, however, wireless messages were received from other liners giving warning of the presence of ice, but the *Titanic*'s Master, Captain Smith, a most experienced sailor, was confident that, by posting two special look-out men in the crow's nest, he would have adequate notice of any icebergs which might be floating on the vessel's route.

Shortly after 11.30 on the night of April 14 one of the look-out men telephoned to the bridge to say he had sighed a large obstruction straight ahead. The first officer, who was on watch, immediately swung the vessel to port, put the engines full speed astern and closed the water-tight doors. But he was too late. In the minute or two which elapsed after the warning had been given, the *Titanic*, which had previously been steaming at twenty-two knots, travelled 500 yards and struck the iceberg a glancing blow. The berg ripped a hole 250 feet long in the vessel's hull and opened five out of the fifteen water-tight compartments. This meant that the ship was doomed, although no one realised this dread fact at the moment of the collision.

Contrary to the view often held about this disaster that a mad scramble for the boats immediately took place, the slight shock that was felt at first caused very little anxiety. Those who were playing cards paused and went on with the game. The only thing that puzzled people was: Why should the ship suddenly stop in mid-ocean? Some of them came up on deck and seeing nothing amiss went back to bed. However, the captain was soon aware that his ship was sinking and he gave the order to uncover and swing out the lifeboats.

His orders were not executed with the promptitude to which we are accustomed today. There had been no boat drill—indeed it was not compulsory at that time—and the men were slow in assembling at their stations, where there was also some confusion. By this time the passengers had been roused by the stewards and helped into their lifebelts. Women and children were ordered to embark first and many did so, but others hesitated at the sight of the boats seventy feet above water. Thus wives refused to leave their husbands and many passengers thought it safer to remain on board, particularly as the lights of another liner could be seen in the distance. Unfortunately the third-class passengers could only reach the boat-deck by two approach ladders and this delayed them; also many of these poor people were reluctant to abandon their possessions in the steerage. Several of the boats were rushed, but several more rowed off without their full complement. Even if full there were insufficient boats to carry more than half the ship's passengers and crew.

Great courage was shown by many on board. For over two hours the stokers worked waist-deep in water to keep the pumps and lights going. Meanwhile the band played on gallantly, at first dance music, and as the end approached 'Nearer, my God, to Thee'. The decks were now awash and the ship was slowing settling. Suddenly she heeled over, her stern rose high out of the water, as she disappeared beneath the waves. The total saved came to little more than 700. The captain and three-quarters of the crew went down with the vessel.

The Board of Trade inquiry into the loss was conducted by Lord Mersey, an experienced Admiralty judge. It lasted for thirty-seven days and during its hearing over one hundred witnesses were examined.

One of these witnesses was Mr. H. A. Sanderson, the manager of the White Star Line. Sir John Simon suggested to him that there should have been lifeboat accommodation for every person on board, but Mr. Sanderson considered that this would have been unwise "because it would have meant hopeless congestion on the boat-deck in an emergency". This witness also made it clear that the Board of Trade regulations in this matter had been faithfully observed. It subsequently transpired that these regulations had not been brought up to date since 1894.

The ship's baker, John Jonghin, in answer to Simon's questions gave a vivid description of the last incidents of the wreck. He described the difficulty of persuading women to enter the lifeboats and how he and other members of the crew had to use force to save the women's lives. "Towards the end," he said, "I went down to my quarters and took a drink.

When I returned to the boat-deck all the lifeboats had gone, but I found a pile of deck-chairs which I flung overboard for swimmers to cling to. Then the ship gave a lurch and hundreds of people were piled on top of one another." When the ship plunged he clung to a rail and suddenly found himself in the icy water. After swimming about for two hours he was picked up by a lifeboat.

There is no doubt that the handling of the case by Simon and his colleagues, in particular the information which Simon elicited from the witnesses, was responsible for the form taken by the court's findings. The court finally held that the high speed and the route chosen were both responsible for the disaster, though the captain was acquitted of any blame in this respect. It found that discipline was good during the lowering of the lifeboats, but it criticised both crew and passengers for the conduct of the boats after the ship went down, holding that several, for fear of being swamped, failed to make the necessary efforts to save the survivors who were in the water. The court did not accept the contention, unlike many of the public, that the first- and second-class passengers had been unduly favoured at the expense of the third class, since so few of the latter were saved. Nor did it believe the charge against one first-class passenger, Sir Cosmo Duff-Gordon, that he bribed the men in his boat to row away from some drowning people.

By his conduct at this inquiry Sir John Simon also contributed to the court's recommendations, which were subsequently put into force in all seagoing merchant vessels. These are, first, that the number of lifeboats carried should be based on the number of persons on board and not, as in the past, on the vessel's tonnage; secondly, that there should be proper lifeboat drill; and thirdly that ships in ice areas should reduce speed at night. In so far as these precautions are now compulsory, some good may be said to have come of the greatest disaster ever to have occurred on the high seas in time of peace.

4. THE KUEPFERLE SPY TRIAL

AS Attorney-General during the First World War, Lord Simon, then Sir John Simon, had to authorise, and in some cases to conduct, the prosecution of German spies. One of the most remarkable of these cases was that of Anton Kuepferle, a man who at first claimed to be an American citizen of Swiss birth, but whom Simon always believed to be a German officer. This particular enemy agent arrived in England early in 1915, posing as a business man from Brooklyn. He gave himself away almost the moment he landed.

Kuepferle's history was interesting. His parents, who were German, had died while he was a boy, and he had consequently been sent to relatives in Brooklyn, where he had been brought up. He worked for a time in a clothing store, and also as a shipping clerk. He then set up in business for himself as a woollen draper, in which undertaking he failed. Finally he took on the New York agency of a Dutch firm of wine merchants.

On the outbreak of war he joined the German Army in commissioned rank and seems to have been at the Front for a time. He then returned to America to join the team of espionage agents being recruited on behalf of the Fatherland by the German Military Attaché in Washington, Captain Franz von Papen, later to become a fateful and notorious figure in the politics of his country.

At the beginning of February, 1915, Kuepferle sailed from New York in the White Star liner *Arabic* as a third-class passenger. His passport described him as an American citizen and stated that he was travelling to England and Holland on business.

On the day his ship reached Liverpool he wrote a letter on notepaper headed 'Küpferle and Co., Importers of Woollens, Brooklyn', and posted it to a certain address in Rotterdam.

Just a few lines to let you know that I have arrived in Liverpool today, and I am expecting to do business by

tomorrow in London. I shall arrive in Rotterdam by the
end of this week, and I hope to have a little rest there until
I am sailing off in a few days. If I could fudge about till I
will be done with my business, you could get me on the
station, but it is very hard to tell. Expecting you are
prepared for me, I remain,

KUEPFERLE.

At this time there was, of course, a postal censorship in
operation in London, and it paid special attention to correspondence directed to neutral countries. Kuepferle's letter
was picked out by an examiner, who was suspicious of its
wording. The censor sent the letter to the chemical laboratory to be tested for possible secret writing. The tests
immediately revealed the existence of a message, which had
been written in invisible ink between the lines of the visible
handwriting.

The message referred to the position, type, and numbers of
warships which the writer had seen in the Irish Channel when
approaching Liverpool. It also revealed details of the equipment and date of departure of a force which was shortly to
leave for the Front. It ended with the words, "I have been up
to the present twice held up for passports and must be quiet
for a while." The reference here seems to indicate that he had
been questioned by immigration or security officers.

Meanwhile, after posting the incriminating letter, Kuepferle
went to Dublin. Two days later he returned to England,
explaining to the passport officer at Holyhead that he was an
American just about to sail for home. Then he went to
London, stayed one night in an hotel near Euston and the
next in another hotel near Victoria.

By this time the police were on his trail and he was arrested.
Among his effects were found two lemons, a bottle of formalin
and, in an inner pocket of his coat, a steel pen.

On May 18, 1915, Kuepferle was arraigned at the Old Bailey
before a specially constituted court, presided over by the Lord
Chief Justice, Lord Reading, and assisted by Mr. Justice Avory
and Mr. Justice Lush. The prisoner was charged with collect-

ing, recording and attempting to communicate information calculated to be useful to the enemy.

He was a typically Teutonic type, tight-lipped, stout, and clean-shaven; in the dock he wore a closely fitting frock-coat and rimless spectacles. He pleaded not guilty, and gave his age as thirty-one, though he looked older. He spoke English with a strong guttural German accent.

The prisoner was defended by Sir Ernest Wild, later Recorder of London. But such was the anti-spy feeling in those days that Sir John Simon, who led the prosecution, had to tell the jury at the outset of the proceedings that defence counsel was only carrying out his professional duty in appearing for the prisoner, and he had to remind them that it was "the proud boast of the English Bar that the help which a barrister could honourably give should not be denied to any man".

In opening the case against Kuepferle Simon also told the jury that, when in Brixton gaol, the prisoner had been given writing-paper so that he could write to his solicitor. He had impudently used this to send a message to a prisoner in an adjoining cell. "The whole of Belgium is in our hands and no longer exists," he wrote in one of these messages. "Oh, if I could only be at the Front again for half an hour."

There were also references to the use of poison gas in Flanders and the fact that he really was a soldier. All very strange statements for an American commercial traveller to express, commented the Attorney-General dryly.

"Now, if you write messages in lemon juice to which formalin has been added," continued the prosecuting counsel, "most schoolboys know that the words become invisible and need to be treated with a re-agent before they can be read."

Kuepferle's letter contained lines which were certainly written in this manner. Not only had the police proved that the nib of his pen had been dipped in this preparation, but one of the lemons, of which the skin was pierced, had also been chemically tested and shown to have been in contact with metal. Incidentally, by an ironic touch, this procedure was known as the 'Prussian blue test'.

In the course of his defence Sir Ernest Wild claimed that the discovery of the lemon and the formalin constituted no proof of the offence with which the prisoner had been charged. "Since formalin is a germicide," he argued, "may it not have been used on his feet for medical purposes?"

Sir John Simon had no difficulty in disposing of this ingenuous plea. "Who ever heard of formalin being applied to the feet with a steel pen?" he asked.

The Attorney-General began his cross-examination of the prisoner with a profoundly pertinent question. "Tell the jury, Mr. Kuepferle," he said, "have you ever been an officer in the German Army?"

The man in the dock stood silent, nervously fingering his lips. Simon repeated the question. Still no answer. "Would you like my question translated into German?" The prisoner shook his head.

Simon turned towards the judge. "With your lordship's permission, I will not press that question now," he said, and then looking steadily at the prisoner he added, "It is my first question, Mr. Kuepferle, but *it will also be my last question*." He then passed on to other matters and had not finished his cross-examination when the court rose for the day.

Early next morning the prisoner was found hanged in his cell. He had tied a scarf round his neck and, with the aid of two library books on which he had stood, had affixed the scarf to the end of the ventilator on the ceiling. He had also written a statement in English on a slate.

In this last message he declared himself to be a native of Baden in Germany and "a soldier with rank", which facts he had not wished to mention before. "I can say that I have had a fair trial of the United Kingdom," he added, "but I am unable to stand the strain any longer and take the law in my own hand."

Thus the Attorney-General's leading question was answered, but in a way that no one in court expected.

THE *TITANIC*

Topical Press

SIR BERNARD SPILSBURY

Picture Press

5. COUNT DE BORCH AND THE UNWRITTEN LAW

DURING the 1914–18 War Sir John Simon conducted the defence at a sensational murder trial which moved the public profoundly. His client, Lieutenant Douglas Malcolm, a young Army officer on active service in France, was charged with the unlawful killing of a man whom he suspected of being his wife's lover. It was about as near as a jury has ever got in an English murder trial to accepting the continental doctrine of the 'unwritten law'.

The man in question was a Polish Jew and a plausible adventurer, whose real name was Anton Baumberg. During his sojourn in this country he posed as a Russian nobleman, having a coronet marked on his gold-mounted umbrella and other possessions and calling himself Count Anthony de Borch. It was an appropriate alias, because that precisely represented his purpose in life, the debauchery of impressionable women. For all his apparent affluence in public, however, he lived in a top-floor back room of a Bayswater boarding-house. He was known to the authorities in Scotland Yard as a white slave trafficker and blackmailer, and he also had connections in the field of German espionage.

In July, 1917, Lieutenant Malcolm came home unexpectedly on leave from France. He found his wife had gone down to a cottage in Hampshire with de Borch and a woman friend of the 'Count's'. Arriving there, Malcolm was shocked at de Borch's seeming intimacy with his wife, so he proceeded to give him a thrashing, "in the good old British way", as Sir John Simon described it. He then took his wife back to London, having first made de Borch promise he would not see her again.

From the railway station he sent him a note challenging him to a duel, and he repeated this challenge before the end of his leave in a letter in which he invited the 'Count' to meet him in France, where duelling was not a criminal offence, as it is in England. De Borch did not reply to either of these invitations.

Although Mrs. Malcolm had also promised not to see the 'Count' again, she broke her word and did so as soon as her husband had gone back to France. At the same time she told Malcolm she could not give up her lover and asked for a divorce.

Malcolm promptly wrote again to de Borch. "If I ever hear of you trying to see or even talk to my wife again," he told him, "wherever I am I will get leave and hunt you out and give you such a thrashing that even your own mother will not know you again."

Alarmed by this communication, the 'Count' bought a revolver, which he showed to Mrs. Malcolm, saying he wanted it in case her husband attacked him.

Fearing the worst, Malcolm obtained compassionate leave from his unit. He reached home and found his wife preparing to go away with de Borch. She had given the servants notice and had got a new travelling trunk with no initials on it.

The husband then went to Scotland Yard, where he discovered the details of de Borch's unsavoury record and found out where he lodged. His next action was to buy a horsewhip, with which he intended to chastise the 'Count'. Before setting out next morning on this mission he wrote a passionate letter to his "very dear, very own darling Dorothy", saying he had discovered de Borch to be the most unutterable blackguard. "I am going to thrash him until he is unrecognisable," he went on. "I may shoot him if he has a gun. I expect he has, as he is too much of a coward to stand a thrashing. If the inevitable has got to happen, I may get it in the neck first."

Malcolm made a will, leaving all his property to his wife's mother in case of his death.

Putting these documents in his pocket with his revolver, Malcolm went to the address in Bayswater where de Borch lodged. The husband told the cook, who opened the door, that he was an inspector from Scotland Yard, and he asked to see the 'Count'. He was shown up to the top back room, where he found de Borch in bed wearing only a pyjama jacket.

As the cook went downstairs she heard a noise. Another woman in the house subsequently swore that she, too, heard sounds as if of a struggle, which lasted for some time. Then reports followed of gunshots being fired.

Malcolm fetched the police, to whom he handed over the weapon with which he admitted having killed de Borch. When the police arrived, they found de Borch's body lying on the bed, and a half-open drawer near-by containing the dead man's revolver.

Malcolm was arrested and charged with murder. He made no attempt to deny his action. "I did it for my honour," he told the police. "You can imagine how I felt when I saw the cad who has been trying to get my wife to go away with him, and *me* in France, helpless to defend her honour! Can you wonder what I did on the spur of the moment, when I saw the cad before me who was luring my wife to dishonour?"

The case was tried by Mr. Justice McCardie at the Old Bailey in September, 1917. Sir Richard Muir, the senior Treasury counsel, conducted the prosecution.

As for the defence, a number of pundits in the Temple considered that the leading brief should not have been given to Sir John Simon, but rather to an experienced criminal lawyer, like Sir Edward Marshall Hall, who would have made an emotional and dramatic appeal to the jury. How wrong they were was demonstrated by the complete success of Simon's tactics throughout this exciting trial.

First of all, Muir was anxious that the prisoner should plead guilty to manslaughter, in which event the murder charge would have been dropped and, in view of the exceptionally strong provocation he had received, the judge would no doubt have bound him over.

But to this course Simon would not agree. He thought the circumstances were such as to get Malcolm clearly absolved from all blame. His case was that the prisoner had acted in self-defence, and he based it on the presence of de Borch's revolver in the room where he was killed.

Next, Sir John Simon took the unusual course of calling no evidence, not even his client. Malcolm was eager to go into the witness-box and describe what he had done, but his counsel adamantly refused to let him do so. He preferred to rely on the effect of his own speech to the jury, and he was rightly unwilling to allow the prisoner to run the risk of spoiling his case.

Speaking in quiet and unemotional tones, Simon began by repudiating any intention of appealing to the 'unwritten law', which in some continental countries permits a husband to kill his wife's lover. "I make no appeal to it," he said. "I do not require to do so; it would be contrary to your duty if you listened to me when I attempted to do so. This is a court of justice, and you are sworn to do justice; and it is justice according to the law, which I stand here to ask you to mete out to Lieutenant Malcolm."

He spoke of his client's marriage, of his joining up on the outbreak of war, of "this black, evil, ugly shadow" which fell across the lives of Douglas Malcolm and his wife, and then of the young husband's frenzy and despair.

"He went to that room to punish and not to kill, and in the struggle which took place it was a choice between de Borch's life and his. He entered that room with that whip for the purpose of giving the man the flogging which he said he would give him, which he had warned him from France he would give him . . . What did he take a whip for else? People bent on using revolvers do not want whips."

Simon paused. Then he turned towards the prisoner and finally towards the jury. "Gentlemen," he said, "Lieutenant Malcolm is here before you in the clothes of a civilian. It is for you to say whether he shall pass from this place to the condemned cell, or whether you . . . will return him to the service of His Majesty, to put on again the uniform which he has done nothing to disgrace and so much to justify."

After a short absence the jury found the prisoner not guilty of either murder or manslaughter. In other words they agreed with Sir John Simon's argument that Lieutenant Malcolm had shot the 'Count' in self-defence.

"Thank God!" exclaimed a woman at the back of the court. Her voice expressed the feeling of the multitude.

6. THE BATH CLUB CASE

IT does not often happen that a reputable London club is concerned in a court action. Disputes which arise within its walls are as a rule settled there, amicably and without publicity. A striking exception was provided by the Bath Club, which was sued by one of its members, Captain Peter Wright, for damages for wrongful expulsion from the club in 1926. Lord Simon, then Sir John Simon, was briefed as leading counsel for the defence in this remarkable action.

The facts which led up to Captain Wright's expulsion from the Bath Club were these. Captain Wright was a journalist and author, who had been educated at Harrow and Balliol College, Oxford. He had recently written a book called *Portraits and Criticisms*, which contained a serious and unsubstantiated charge against the private character of William Ewart Gladstone, the Liberal statesman, who had been four times Prime Minister of Britain. It was to the effect that Mr. Gladstone was accustomed "in public to speak the language of the highest and strictest principle and in private to pursue and possess every sort of woman". This was a novel and hideous construction on the Liberal leader's well-known interest in reclaiming fallen women from the streets. Incidentally, the publishers stated that the offensive passage was not in the original manuscript of the book as accepted by them and must have been written by the author afterwards.

A copy of the book fell into the hands of Gladstone's family. Accordingly, the statesman's sons, Lord Gladstone and Mr. H. N. Gladstone, wrote to Captain Wright at the club describing what he had written as 'garbage'. Their letter continued, "You are a liar. Because you slander a dead man, you are a coward. Because you think that the public will accept invention from such as you, you are a fool."

Captain Wright replied on club notepaper, amplifying the original attack. He declared that he wrote what he did write on the authority of the late Lord Milner, who had stated, according to Captain Wright, that Gladstone was "governed by his seraglio".

Captain Wright sent both letters to the newspapers. Later Lord Gladstone wrote inviting Captain Wright to take proceedings against him. "The public will form its own judgment," he said, "if you decline to take the only course consistent with honour and truth—an action against us in a court of law."

This letter needs a word of explanation. Unlike some continental countries, a libel on a dead person is not actionable in the English courts at the suit of the dead man's family. Hence Lord Gladstone hoped that Captain Wright might be provoked into suing him and his brother for the defamatory remarks contained in their first letter. But Captain Wright declined to take any steps in this sense on the ground that there had been technically no 'publication' of the Gladstones' letter to a third party as legally required to sustain a civil action for libel.

The secretary of the Bath Club now wrote to Captain Wright objecting to his use of the club notepaper in his correspondence with Lord Gladstone. The only relevant club rule, however, was one prohibiting members from using its address for advertisements.

Eventually the committee met, with the chairman, Lord Desborough, in the chair, and came to the conclusion that Captain Wright's failure to take action against Lord Gladstone showed that he admitted his conduct as alleged, and that this conduct was consequently injurious to the character and interests of the club. Captain Wright's expulsion was accordingly decided on, but the offending member was informed of the meeting only after the decision to expel him had been taken; he was not invited to attend for the purpose of stating his own case. Captain Wright promptly issued a writ against the club.

The action was heard before Mr. Justice Horridge and a special jury in the King's Bench Division in July, 1926. Mr. St. John Field, later a county court judge, appeared for the plaintiff. For the defence, Sir John Simon had with him Mr. William Jowitt, now Lord Jowitt.

After Mr. Field had opened the case for his client, the judge intervened with a remark which went to the root of the matter.

"The issue for the jury," said Mr. Justice Horridge, "is simply whether Captain Wright was condemned unheard. If so, there is no defence to this action."

It is a principle of British justice that no person shall be penalised until he has had an opportunity of putting forward his side of the case, and it was clear from Captain Wright's evidence that he had not been provided in this instance with such an opportunity.

Sir John Simon was therefore faced with a formidable task when he rose to cross-examine the plaintiff. He realised that he could not effectively challenge the facts as related by Captain Wright. The details of Gladstone's private morality were, of course, largely beside the point for the purposes of this action. The most that Simon could hope for would be to minimise the claim for damages in respect of the club's breach of contract with Captain Wright resulting in his loss of the club's amenities. There was also a claim for injury to the plaintiff's reputation. Here the damages awarded might conceivably be considerable. Simon therefore set to work to attack the plaintiff.

"Is the Bath Club a club for both men and women?" was Simon's first question. The plaintiff said it was. Here the judge again interrupted. "Well," he said, "it does not comply with the Bishop's definition of a man's club as a place 'where the women cease from troubling and the weary are at rest'." A ripple of laughter ran round the court at this judicial sally.

"Do you take the view," continued Simon, "that every man on two legs is a gentleman for the purpose of the Bath Club?" The witness replied he did not understand this question.

Simon proceeded to elaborate it by asking whether it was not injurious to the interests of the club to have a member who notoriously behaved not like a gentleman but like a cad.

Captain Wright was bound to agree that if the man was a proved cad, he was a menace to any club. Then, said Simon, look at the twenty-two distinguished members of the committee who had voted for his expulsion. Were they not competent judges? Captain Wright, however, did not agree. One of the committee men he described as being "far too stupid" to be a judge of anything. In his opinion, the witness declared,

79

the committee represented "money, athletics and snobbery", and nothing else.

Simon also forced the plaintiff to admit that the statement that Gladstone "was governed by his seraglio" was not used in its original context in the sense in which it had been subsequently employed by Captain Wright to bolster up his accusation. These words had really referred to "the devoted wife and daughter who looked after the comforts of the great Liberal leader".

So as to have the last word with the jury, Simon called no evidence. In his final speech he suggested that a farthing damages would give Captain Wright "just about a farthing more than he is worth". The plaintiff, he said, was claiming damages for loss of reputation, but he had failed to satisfy the test of a gentleman, for no gentleman would broadcast on inadequate grounds deeply injurious statements about a man recently dead. He summarised the difficult position with which the Bath Club had to deal, and ended by urging that it might be very hard for the committee of a social club always to act in perfectly precise accordance with its rules and this committee had discharged their duty as they understood it.

The jury found that Captain Wright had been condemned unheard. They awarded him £100 damages for loss of the Bath Club's amenities and £25 for loss of reputation.

The judge observed that it had never been decided whether damages under the second head were recoverable in cases of this sort and he would require to hear counsel's argument on that point. But Sir John Simon did not think it worth while to argue the point for the sake of a mere £25. So it remains unsettled.

7. THE PORTUGUESE BANKNOTE CASE

"I AM not going to yield to the temptation to become the Edgar Wallace of the Law Courts, though I realise it would be a popular part." With these words Sir John Simon opened his last big case in 1931 before leaving the Bar for good. Nevertheless, the story he unfolded in the Court of Appeal on this occasion seemed almost fantastic; it might well have come from the pages of a detective thriller. It involved the fabrication and distribution throughout Portugal of false banknotes to the face value of more than £1,000,000. The notes were printed in London, but so ingenious was the deception practised that only the printers could tell the difference between genuine notes of the same denomination and those which were in effect forgeries.

The story begins on December 4, 1924. On that day a Dutchman, who gave his name as Mr. K. Marang Van Ysselveere, of The Hague, presented himself at the offices of Waterlow's, the well-known firm of printers in the City. He looked about thirty-five years old and, in the words used by Sir John Simon in court, was "an ingratiating foreigner with beautiful manners". Mr. Marang carried with him a letter of introduction from a firm of printers of high standing in Holland addressed to Sir William Waterlow, the chairman of the English firm. The letter stated that its bearer wished to place an order for the printing of banknotes which might best be executed by Waterlow's. Incidentally, Waterlow's had previously printed notes for the Bank of Portugal.

Mr. Marang explained that the finances of the Portuguese colony of Angola were in a bad way, and that a Dutch syndicate of which he was a member was, at the request of the Portuguese Government, going to the colony's assistance. The syndicate proposed to subscribe £1,000,000 sterling and the Bank of Portugal was prepared to help. Marang accordingly asked if Waterlows would print some of the Bank's notes for circulation in Angola. After delivery the notes would be overprinted in the colony with the word 'Angola' on their face. The High Commissioner was leaving for the colony in about two months' time and would take the notes with him, the plausible Mr. Marang went on, so that there was no time to be lost. He added that the matter must be treated as strictly confidential.

Sir William Waterlow naturally asked for time to consider the proposition and an appointment was made for about a fortnight later. On this occasion Marang brought with him various legal documents which had been duly authenticated by a Portuguese notary. One of them was a contract by which the Bank of Portugal seemingly authorised the Government of Angola to arrange for the printing of the notes.

Sir William Waterlow informed the visitor that his firm could not supply the notes without the authority of the Bank, since it owned the plates from which the printing was done. He would, therefore, write to the Bank for their authority, which, after consulting his colleagues and having also taken legal advice, he was satisfied would put the matter in order.

Mr. Marang, who said he happened to be going to Lisbon next day, offered to take the letter with him, and to this Sir William Waterlow agreed.

Marang returned to London a few weeks later, bringing with him a reply purporting to be signed by the Governor of the Bank. It was written on notepaper bearing the Portuguese national arms in the corner, and though it was not the kind of paper which the Bank used, its style was sufficient to impress Waterlows. It contained the necessary authority and requested the British firm to deal directly with Marang on matters of detail. It was, however, written in English and not Portuguese, in which language the Bank had previously communicated with Waterlows. Also the seals were different from those formerly used. These points escaped attention at the time, and the bogus letter was accepted and acted upon by Waterlows in good faith.

Waterlows now set to work to fill the order. Two hundred thousand notes in denominations of 500 escudos (approximately £5) came off the printing presses as a first instalment. Each note bore the portrait of Vasco da Gama, the great Portuguese navigator, and to all except the expert eye of Waterlows themselves were identical in appearance with the notes previously printed by Waterlows for the Bank.

Early in February, 1925, Marang took delivery of the consignment, collecting the notes in a large suitcase, which he subsequently deposited for the night in the cloak-room of Liverpool Street station. An even larger printing, some 380,000 notes, was executed by the firm some months later. None of the notes ever reached Angola. But the equivalent of more than £1,000,000 passed into circulation in Portugal.

To facilitate this process the conspirators, who included a brother of the Portuguese Minister in The Hague, obtained permission for the Ministry of Finance in Lisbon to found a new bank, the Bank of Angola, and it was through its medium that the bulk of the false notes reached the public.

But gradually suspicions were aroused. Eventually, the police searched the Bank of Angola premises in Oporto and found several large bundles of new Vasco da Gama notes, which were neither numbered nor packed in accordance with the practice of the Bank of Portugal.

On December 5, 1925, the Bank of Portugal suddenly decided to withdraw the whole Vasco da Gama issue from circulation. The public were allowed three weeks to exchange any of the notes for others, after which they would become valueless.

The directors did not cable Waterlows until a week or so later, and though Sir William Waterlow immediately hurried to Lisbon to explain how the spurious notes could be distinguished from the genuine ones—a magnifying glass revealed a small letter on the stalk of the lily in the design, which did not appear on the plate previously used—the bank insisted on carrying out the withdrawal *in toto*.

This naturally involved a great rush on the bank and greatly increased the measure of damages subsequently claimed against Waterlows. Meanwhile, Marang and his associates were arrested, tried and sentenced to terms of imprisonment.

In the King's Bench Division in London, in January, 1931, the Bank obtained judgment against Waterlows for £570,000, the amount of the face value of the notes less certain deductions. Both sides appealed—Waterlows on the ground that the damages awarded were excessive, and the Bank on the grounds that they were not enough. Sir John Simon conducted the appeal on behalf of Waterlows.

At the outset he admitted that his clients could not escape some measure of liability in that they had not used reasonable care to prevent the fraud. But he strongly urged that when the Bank called in the Vasco da Gama issue, it need not have exchanged the false notes, the majority of which could have been recognised by the special printers' mark. "It seems an astonishing thing," he said, "for the directors to get round a table and, because they could not see any difference between the authorised notes and the false notes, to decide to withdraw the whole issue. If instead they had immediately telegraphed Messrs. Waterlows they would have received information regarding the means of identifying the notes which would have been of the greatest value."

Then came the most interesting and ingenious part of his argument. Yes, he said, the Bank had been involved in loss, but this was in reality quite small—the mere cost of printing new notes to replace the Vasco da Gama issue which it had withdrawn. In England, said Simon, things were different. Here, at least in theory, the holder of a banknote could demand gold for it. But in Portugal, where the currency had for long been inconvertible, a banknote could be exchanged only for another banknote.

Finally, Sir John Simon agreed that the extra notes issued had caused some inflation in Portugal, but he argued that the loss thereby caused fell on the public who held the currency and not on the bank.

Only Lord Justice Scrutton, the President of the Court of Appeal, accepted Sir John Simon's argument in its entirety. His two colleagues held that the damages should be reduced to £300,000.

Both sides then went to the House of Lords. By this time Sir John Simon had become Foreign Secretary, so that he was unable to take any part in the ultimate appeal. Whether his arguments would have convinced the highest court, of which he was later such a distinguished member, is a matter for speculation. The fact remains that the Law Lords not merely reversed the judgment of the Court of Appeal, but awarded the Bank the huge sum of £610,000, which they had originally claimed.

III. LAW AND CRIME

III. LAW AND CRIME

1. SIR PATRICK HASTINGS

A SUCCESSFUL barrister can as a rule either convince judges or sway juries. He can rarely do both, though occasionally, like the first Lord Reading and the first Lord Birkenhead, he does succeed in combining profound knowledge of the law with moving eloquence. Broadly speaking, however, barristers may be classified either as lawyers or else as advocates. Into the latter category falls Sir Patrick Hastings, perhaps the last survivor of the great school of advocacy in our Courts of Justice.

If he did not achieve the highest prizes in his profession, 'Pat' Hastings was undoubtedly an outstanding and versatile leader of the Bar; as 'Pat' he is still affectionately remembered by friends and colleagues in the Temple. After humble beginnings and hard struggles in his early days, he entered Parliament and became the first Labour Attorney-General at the age of forty-four. He also served in three wars, and as a playwright scored several well-deserved successes in the West End. But it is as an advocate in the courts that he is especially remembered. He might have gone on the Bench; he preferred to remain an advocate to the end of his professional career.

I first saw him when I was a Bar student, and not long afterwards I was 'called' to the Bar by him in his capacity as Treasurer of the Middle Temple. It was at the time of his dramatic defence of Mrs. Barney, whose acquittal was secured in 1932 on a charge of murdering her lover. The case had a particular interest for me as some time previously I had met the unfortunate young man who lost his life at Mrs. Barney's hands—by accident, as the jury subsequently found. I was immensely impressed by Sir Patrick's advocacy in that sordid and sensational case. I made a point of attending courts when I knew he was appearing, so as to observe his methods with juries and witnesses. In cross-examination he would seize on one point, the significance of which was usually not appreciated by anyone else at the outset of the trial, and hammer it home relentlessly.

The trial of Mrs. Barney provided a good illustration of this technique. The principal Crown witness, a woman neighbour of Mrs. Barney's at the time of the shooting, had stated in her examination-in-chief that the prisoner had shouted after her lover as he was leaving her mews flat "I will shoot you". Under cross-examination by Sir Patrick this witness admitted that she might have been mistaken and the words could have been "I will shoot". The difference seemed very slight, but it was vital, since if those were the words actually used, they might be consistent with the prisoner's threat to shoot herself. This was the line that Mrs. Barney herself took when she went into the box, and the jury believed her.

Later when I got to know Sir Patrick personally and we discussed some of his cases together, he told me he had modelled his own style of advocacy on that of the late Lord Carson. "He was by far the greatest advocate I have ever known," he once said to me. "He had the power of convincing his tribunal not only that his cause was just but that his client was as honest as his advocate. His power of cross-examination was not an art, it was simply natural genius. Whether his task was long or short he never wasted a word; he knew what he wanted to achieve and he never stopped until he had achieved it, but no one has ever suggested that he asked one superfluous question." This gift was, I think, the secret of Patrick Hastings success as it was of Edward Carson's.

From the beginning it was an uphill struggle for 'Pat' Hastings. His parents were able to give him a decent schooling and he was sent to Charterhouse, but he was taken away at the age of sixteen because his father could not afford to keep him there any longer. His first job was working as a navvy on an engineering site in North Wales at a wage of 30/- a week. After eighteen months he enlisted and fought as a trooper in the South African War. Then came a spell as a journalist in Fleet Street, while reading for the Bar and saving up the 100

SIR PATRICK HASTINGS

guineas necessary to become a barrister. Then came the great day of his 'call' at the Middle Temple and the start of his legal career. That was in 1904.

He waited for briefs, but they did not come, at least not in numbers to keep body and soul together. He wrote a little text-book on the law of money-lending and went on waiting. His first case was a nerve-racking experience. Indeed for a long time afterwards he suffered from nervousness in an acute form whenever he had to get up in court. In 1906 he got married. Then the tide began to turn. In that year he earned £200. Mr. Horace Avory, K.C., later the famous judge, took him as the only other occupant of his chambers in Crown Office Row. He secured the services of Avory's clerk, an invaluable asset, and his practice increased. His first really lucrative brief, marked at what was for him in those days the unbelievable sum of 400 guineas, arrived as the result of a strange accident.

Mr. Montague Shearman, K.C., was retained to defend a rich prisoner at Maidstone Assizes. His junior counsel was named Hart. Shortly before the trial was due to come on it was discovered that Hart was not a member of the South-Eastern Circuit, and the rule of all circuits is that there must be a 'circuit junior' in every case. The solicitors picked up the current Law List and found that the next circuit member whose name appeared there was Hastings. So Hastings got the brief. Unfortunately when the brief was delivered he was laid up in bed with an attack of chicken-pox. However, he was determined to appear and, disguising his spots with a liberal application of Fuller's earth, he made his way to Maidstone. Then the miracle happened. He found the Grand Jury had thrown out the case, and so he was free to go back to bed with the comforting knowledge that the fat brief fee was safely lodged in his bank.

His big chance came in a libel action in which he was being led by Sir Edward Carson. It was brought by Robert Sievier, the race-horse owner, against Richard Wootton, the trainer. Sievier had been prosecuted for blackmail in 1908 and in common parlance had 'got away with it'. Not long afterwards

Wootton alleged that his acquittal was entirely unjustified. At the end of the second day the plaintiff had yet to be cross-examined. Normally Carson would have done this, but at the rising of the court he told his junior that he had been urgently called away to Ulster—the Home Rule controversy was at its height—and he left the task to his junior. Hastings was over-joyed, but at the same time more than a little anxious. However, he succeeded in showing up Bob Sievier for the rogue that he was; Sievier lost his action and the racing world knew him no more.

"When Carson went to Ulster that night," Sir Patrick told me, "he brought me fortune." Henceforward there was to be no lack of work. In 1919 he became a K.C. and for the next thirty years he was at the top of the tree as an advocate. In 1924 he received the customary knighthood on becoming a Law Officer in the first Ramsay MacDonald Government. Unfortunately his brief excursion into politics brought him only bitterness and disillusion. He was back in private practice, having shaken the dust of Westminster off his feet, long before Mr. MacDonald became Prime Minister for the second time in 1929.

Of the celebrated cases which he conducted during the period of his eminence, it is difficult to say which was his greatest. He conducted them all brilliantly. His defence of Mrs. Barney and Jean Pierre Vaquier on charges of murder are, I think, especially noteworthy, as also his defence of Mr. Harold Morland, the accountant in the Lord Kylsant case, who was acquitted on the charge of conniving at the issue of fraudulent balance sheets by the Chairman of the Royal Mail Steam Packet Company. In the civil field his appearance in the famous Diamond Syndicate case in 1930 must occupy a very high place. There were over 4,000 documents in this complicated case, which concerned the secret workings of the diamond industry. Such a mass of documents led to the intro-duction of much irrelevant matter and tended to confuse the jury. Sir Patrick concentrated his cross-examination on eliciting from a key witness one small fact, which he considered vital. It was a risk, which his clients were opposed to his taking, but it came off and he won.

The last case in which I heard him in court was the action for libel brought by the late Professor Harold Laski against a number of newspapers who reported the Professor as advocating revolution and violence during the General Election of 1945, when he appeared for the defendants. It was his last big case and he was on the winning side. His vigorous advocacy seemed to be unimpaired, but unknown to the onlooker the machine was running down. Soon afterwards he suffered an illness and decided to retire.

His retirement gave him leisure to write another play, which was later made into a successful film. He called it *The Blind Goddess*, after the blindfold figure of Justice holding her evenly-balanced scales above the Old Bailey. It was an aptly chosen title. No one has served the blind goddess more faithfully and few so well throughout a full and varied career as an advocate than Patrick Hastings.

2. THE LAST OF THE SERJEANTS

AS a Bar student twenty years ago, my favourite activity was to cross the Strand from the Temple to the Law Courts and listen to the cases being tried there.

The first time I went into court as a spectator I noticed a tall, bearded figure who sat in the front row with the other King's Counsel, spoke with a charming Irish brogue and, unlike his colleagues, wore a wig with a round piece of black silk attached to it.

The piece of silk denoted the wearer's peculiar rank at the Bar—that of serjeant-at-law. The advocate who captivated my attention was Serjeant Sullivan, whose memoirs have now been published.* He was the last of his kind to practise at the English Bar.

The serjeants formerly were an order of the highest rank of barristers. But after the fusion of the various old courts into the High Court of Justice in 1873 no more serjeants were appointed in England. It was otherwise in Ireland, where they

---

* *The Last Serjeant. The Memoirs of Serjeant A. M. Sullivan, Q.C.* (1952).

were seen in the courts until the creation of the Irish Free State in 1922.

Serjeant Sullivan, who had been appointed while at the Irish Bar, found it impossible to continue practice in Ireland during the troubled period which preceded the final break with England. At the age of fifty he came to London and started practice anew.

Alexander Martin Sullivan was the son of A. M. Sullivan, an Irish Nationalist M.P. He was brought up in New York, where as a youth he worked on newspapers, and married a Brooklyn girl. He returned to Ireland in 1892 to be called to the Irish Bar and to practise there with considerable success for more than a quarter of a century.

One of his stories concerns a Recorder of Cork who went in for Latin quotations.

"Mr. Barry," said the Recorder on one occasion, "has your client never heard the maxim *sic utere tuo ut alienum non lædas*?"

"Not a day passes, your honour, on which he does not hear it," replied the imperturbable counsel. "It is the sole topic of conversation where he lives at the top of Mushera Mountain."

Until 1916 Serjeant Sullivan was virtually unknown in England. In that year he came prominently into the limelight through his spirited and ingenious defence of Sir Roger Casement on a charge of high treason at the Old Bailey.

Casement had been landed in a German submarine at a wild spot on the west coast of Ireland on the eve of the Sinn Fein rising in Easter week. Serjeant Sullivan asserts that, far from coming to promote rebellion, Casement's mission was designed to stop it.

Serjeant Sullivan also comments on Casement's private diary, which fell into the hands of the British authorities and showed that he was addicted to homosexual practices. The diary was not in evidence at the trial and, though it was offered for his inspection by the Home Office, Serjeant Sullivan declined to read it.

Serjeant Sullivan reveals for the first time that the Attorney-General, F. E. Smith (later Lord Birkenhead), who was in charge of the prosecution in the Casement trial, was anxious that the leading defence counsel should plead 'guilty but insane' on behalf of his client. The serjeant held the view that there was no insanity and that to attempt to give the Crown an excuse for reprieve—to placate American opinion—by publishing the horrible diary would have been a betrayal of the accused. And so the law took its course and Casement was hanged.

Besides describing many of his cases in both countries, Serjeant Sullivan has some pertinent things to say about the administration of English justice.

In his view it is still far too expensive. Irish justice, he says, was, and still is, about one-fifth the cost of English justice though largely identical in practice. He also thinks English law is too technical and archaic, and he is by no means happy about the state of the law of evidence. He dislikes the habit of two or more accused persons being tried together when, of course, evidence against one is legally not evidence against the other. But the jury find it very difficult to dismiss it from their minds when arriving at a verdict.

The most jovial and attractive criminal with whom Serjeant Sullivan ever came in contact was the financier Ernest Terah Hooley. He tells how a young man who had parted with £2,000 for one of Hooley's bogus ventures called at the financier's fine country house near Derby, determined to get his money back.

The financier invited the visitor to come in and have some lunch, which he did. He was also given several glasses of wine. When the young man left he had parted with a further £3,000. Hooley thought this was a huge joke and laughed uproariously when the story was later put to him in the witness-box.

Serjeant Sullivan has retired from the Bar and lives in Dublin. By the legal profession in this country the last of the serjeants is remembered for his kindliness, gaiety, wit, courage and good fellowship.

3. THE CRIME DOCTOR

IN the field of crime there is one name which has become almost legendary in this country. It is that of Spilsbury. By the general public Sir Bernard Spilsbury is remembered as the greatest medical detective of this century, whose work has brought retribution to scores of notorious murderers.

In professional circles he was regarded during his lifetime as a most gifted and painstaking pathologist, who raised the practice of forensic medicine to the highest level in the achievement of criminal investigation.

An authoritative account of this remarkable man and his career had been eagerly awaited from the time of his death. It appeared with the publication of a biography based on his unpublished papers, including the card indexes of all the case histories which he compiled as Home Office pathologist.*

When Bernard Spilsbury went to work in St. Mary's Hospital as a medical student in 1899, many doctors still spoke of morbid anatomy and pathology as 'a beastly science'. It was the gift of a new microscope from his father, a wholesale chemist from Leamington, that attracted the young man to the post-mortem room, where he followed the forbidden practice of taking home small specimens for examination with his own instrument.

On becoming qualified he was appointed assistant pathologist on the staff of this hospital. A few years later, at the age of thirty-three, came the turning point in his career.

This was in 1910, when he was called in by the authorities to analyse the remains of a woman which had been discovered in the cellar of a house in North London. The dead woman was Mrs. Cora Crippen, who had been poisoned by her husband and whose dissected body had subsequently been buried by him in lime.

Spilsbury's evidence did much to send the poisoner Crippen to the gallows. It also made the young pathologist a national figure, and was the beginning of his long professional association with the Home Office and with the coroners' courts.

During the next thirty-seven years he carried out 25,000 post-mortems. Only a small proportion of these had to do with murder, perhaps 250, but it is upon these that his reputation as

* *Bernard Spilsbury. His Life and Cases.* By Douglas G. Browne and E. V. Tullett (1951).

a public figure rests. Indeed, there were few murder cases between 1911 and his death in 1947 at which he did not give expert evidence.

It was therefore not unnatural that his pronouncements in the witness-box should sometimes have assumed a semblance of infallibility with juries, and that the resultant verdicts should have been attacked in consequence by arm-chair detectives.

This was particularly noticeable in the trial of Norman Thorne for the murder of Elsie Cameron in 1925, when Spilsbury's evidence as the sole expert witness for the Crown was preferred by the jury to the testimony of five doctors for the defence, led by Spilsbury's voluble but much less skilled professional rival, Dr. Brontë.

The leading criminal judge of his time, Sir Travers Humphreys, regarded Spilsbury as the ideal scientific witness.

"He was unemotional," Sir Travers has recalled, "simple in speech because he was clear in mind, absolutely fair, quite indifferent to the result of a case.

"He spared no pains in seeking out anything, fact, theory, or latest discovery, which could properly affect his judgment."

It was precisely because he disdained the use of guess-work that Spilsbury built up such a brilliant reputation for himself, which invariably withstood the most rigorous cross-examination.

Even when conducting a post-mortem on the body of an executed criminal, he took the same pains as he did with his other cases, and his examination frequently lasted an hour or more. Incidentally he was most interested in the effects of judicial hanging, and his realisation that the cervical spine could be broken at a more or less constant level led to an increase of three inches in the drop on humanitarian grounds as a result of his recommendation.

The figure which emerges from a study of his life and cases is that of a kindly, sympathetic character, actuated by an unswerving fidelity to truth and justice.

He possessed a fine sense of humour, though he occasionally indulged in a grim jest. There is a story that in his younger days he carried home part of a human leg, on which he had been working, and left it under a dish-cover in the kitchen to test the reactions of the cook. They were violent.

Another characteristic was his defective sense of smell, about which some good stories are also told. On one occasion he attended the graveside for an exhumation dressed in his usual immaculate manner and wearing a top hat. When the coffin was raised, he ran his nose along it, straightened himself, and remarked, "Arsenic, gentlemen."

At a post-mortem following another exhumation, a young C.I.D. officer, whose first experience of this kind it was, lit a cigarette to steady his nerves. Presently Spilsbury came into the mortuary. He sniffed twice and, looking round the room, said, "You mustn't smoke, please; I can't smell the smells I want to smell." He then bent over the corpse and, according to the officer, was soon sniffing away as if it were a rose-garden.

Of his many difficult cases, Spilsbury considered that the most difficult was the Crumbles murder in 1923. At its outset the police thought they had a very poor case against the accused, Patrick Mahon.

It was Spilsbury who built it up like a jig-saw puzzle and eventually secured Mahon's conviction. This case was also the most shocking in Spilsbury's long experience. Inured as he was to horrors, Spilsbury had to admit that the human remains discovered in the bungalow at the Pevensey end of the Crumbles were the most gruesome he had ever seen.

Spilsbury lived almost entirely for his work. Yet to its material rewards he was indifferent. His fees were always much lower than he might have charged—his Home Office appointment was honorary—and the necessity of making money against the day of his retirement drove him to overwork and thus impaired his health.

His later years, too, were clouded by domestic tragedy. One son was killed in an air raid during the war, and another died of galloping consumption. These losses wrought a deep change in Spilsbury. Life for him now no longer seemed worth living. He had severe attacks of mental depression.

His last post-mortem in a murder case was carried out in 1947 on the body of Alec de Antiquis, who was shot dead by three young ruffians who had carried out a jewel robbery in broad daylight, and whose escape the dead man had obstructed. In the same year Spilsbury suffered a stroke and realised that his powers were declining.

One evening, a few months later, a colleague passing Spilsbury's laboratory in University College, Gower Street, saw a light coming through the fanlight over the door and smelled gas. He knocked and received no answer. When the nightwatchman eventually opened the door with his pass-key it was clear that what had happened was no accident. Artificial respiration was tried without success.

Thus the man who had conducted so many thousands of post-mortems was eventually the subject of one himself. The primary cause of death was given as coronary thrombosis; the secondary cause as carbon monoxide poisoning.

4. WERE THEY WRONG TO FIND HIM GUILTY?

SHOULD Ronald True ever have been found guilty? His death in 1951, after twenty-eight years' detention in Broadmoor Criminal Lunatic Asylum, recalls one of the most controversial murders of our times. The reprieve granted by the Home Secretary, the late Mr. Edward Shortt, raised a storm throughout the country which at one moment threatened the continuance in office of Mr. Lloyd George's Government.

Ronald True was a wastrel, a petty thief, a drug addict, and finally a murderer. He was arrested on the evening of March 6, 1922, while seated with a friend in a box at the Hammersmith Palace of Varieties. He was later charged with the murder of Olive Young a young woman of easy virtue, with whom he had spent the previous night at her flat in Fulham.

His trial took place before Mr. Justice McCardie at the Old Bailey in May. The prosecution for the Crown was led by the late Sir Richard Muir, assisted by Mr. Eustace Fulton. The prisoner was defended by the late Sir Henry Curtis-Bennett and Mr. Roland Oliver, now Mr. Justice Oliver.

The fact of the killing was not denied. The only issue before

97

the jury was whether the defence could substantiate a plea of insanity. And in this event whether True could be enabled to escape the scaffold.

Hitherto the prisoner's life story had been a squalid one. Since childhood he had been regarded as eccentric. He had drifted about the world living on money provided by his mother. When in New York he had married an actress, who had a child by him. For years he had been addicted to morphia. Somehow he became an officer in the Royal Flying Corps during the First World War. But he never saw any foreign service: he crashed a training airplane at Farnborough, which gave him severe concussion of the brain.

If a person commits an offence when he is in an insane condition the verdict of the jury must be that he is 'guilty but insane'. Unfortunately the law is not clear as to what constitutes legal insanity. It was here that the judge brought his undoubted legal genius to bear on the complexities of the case. "I want you to realise that if a man be not absolutely insane within the meaning of the English law," Mr. Justice McCardie told the jury, "it is usual that the jury should vindicate the law with iron firmness."

The law about insanity was originally laid down at the McNaughten trial in 1843, when Daniel McNaughten was convicted for the killing of Mr. Drummond, private secretary to the Prime Minister, Sir Robert Peel, and that law prevails today. It amounts to this. Insanity will only be entertained as an excuse where the accused person can show that his aberration of mind was such that he did not know what he was doing, *or, if he did know what he was doing, did not know that it was wrong*. It is thus assumed that if a man does wrong knowing it to be wrong, he could have refrained from doing it and must consequently be taken to realise the consequences of his act.

There was abundant evidence at the trial to show that True was insane. Nevertheless, the jury found him guilty and he was sentenced to death. Verdict and sentence were confirmed by the Court of Criminal Appeal.

Then the Home Secretary stepped in. By the Criminal

Lunatics Act 1884, Mr. Shortt was bound to order an inquiry by a commission of three doctors. These medical men were all authorities on mental disease, and they unanimously endorsed the expert evidence given at the trial, thus finding that True was an undoubted lunatic. This being so, the Home Secretary had no alternative under the statute but to order a respite. For this action he was violently assailed both in Parliament and in the country. The True case demonstrated that the law of England in relation to criminal insanity is a mass of anomalies. The distinction between medical insanity and criminal insanity (i.e. moral irresponsibility) is a confusing one, particularly to a jury, and many experts think it should be abolished.

I have no doubt the Home Secretary's decision in this case was correct both on legal and moral grounds. But the question arises: Should Ronald True ever have been found guilty at all?

The late Lord Birkenhead, when Lord Chancellor, recommended that a person charged criminally with an offence is irresponsible for his act when the act is committed under an impulse which he was by mental disease in substance deprived of any power to resist. Ronald True unquestionably fell into this category. Meanwhile he has at last died a natural death. But the country is still waiting for the necessary parliamentary legislation to bring Lord Birkenhead's wise recommendation into effect.

5. METROPOLITAN POLICEWOMAN

TODAY the Metropolitan policewoman is taken for granted as part of our daily life, like her uniformed counterpart in the women's services of the armed forces. But this has not always been so. When the first women police appeared in the London streets in 1919, with their unimaginative uniforms and impossible boots, they were an embarrassing target of ridicule. Passers-by stopped to stare and giggle.

At first, too, their male colleagues resented their presence in the force. They had to patrol in pairs, their hours of duty being limited to the afternoon and evening, and the men had strict orders to keep them always in sight, and to rush immediately to their assistance should it become necessary. Nor had the women police any powers of arrest. Their main task was to help in curbing prostitution in the West End. Yet reluctance was shown in putting them into the witness-box in Magistrates' Courts to supply the corroborative evidence necessary in soliciting charges. For a long time male police preferred to put each other into the box for this purpose rather than the women.

Slowly but surely, however, the new branch of the force began to make its way, and by the mid-twenties its members were rendering a real service to the community. Their clothing and equipment were designed in more rational lines, their work gradually came to be appreciated throughout the force, and their sphere of duties as well as their powers were extended, so that they eventually became an invaluable link between all classes of female offenders, real and potential, and the various welfare organisations charged with the after-care of women and children. Their services were also utilised to advantage in the Criminal Investigation Department at Scotland Yard.

For instance, it was a woman member of this branch who began the inquiries into the disappearance of Mrs. Durand-Deacon in 1949 from the Kensington hotel where she lived. This woman detective interviewed John George Haigh, who was staying in the same hotel, and was immediately struck by his plausibility and shiftiness. Her prompt action and subsequent report to her superiors resulted in the arrest and conviction of a notorious murderer who had made away with at least half a dozen victims by the 'acid bath' process.

It was a woman police constable who, in the years between the two world wars, was the means of unmasking a dope-peddling ring by a method which no male member of the force could have followed. The authorities had reason to suspect that cocaine was being distributed in the large public lavatories used by women in the Piccadilly, Leicester Square and Charing Cross districts. The drug-purveyors thought that their traffic could never be detected in these places, set apart as they are for women's exclusive use. It never occurred to them that a woman could keep observation as well as a man. And so it proved to be.

The woman police constable detailed for this duty, for which she naturally wore ordinary clothes, made friends with the prostitutes, who are the principal customers of these establishments, where they frequently repair to wash, change, 'make up' and gossip. To such an extent did the constable win these women's confidence that she agreed temporarily to 'work the beat' of one of them, who happened to be serving a short prison sentence. With considerable tact and astuteness she kept up the pretence until at last the day came for which she had waited for many weeks. She was offered, and bought, a tiny packet of cocaine. She immediately returned to her patrol in another part of London, the peddlers and distributors were rounded up, and a dangerous drug racket was broken.

The details of this and other achievements of the Metropolitan women police are told in an interesting book.* The author, Miss Lilian Wyles, was one of the original members of the force in 1919, and of her thirty years service she spent twenty-seven with the C.I.D. Her book is a well written and finely balanced account of the early struggles and achievements of this women's force.

Miss Wyles described many of the cases in which she participated, including the celebrated Thompson-Bywaters murder, and the so-called 'Case of the Horse with the Green Tail', a shocking rape committed at the Horse Guards by a number of guardsmen on a fourteen-year-old girl in 1938. Miss Wyles subsequently received repeated requests to make arrangements for the termination of this girl's pregnancy, to which she very properly replied that this was outside the scope of her work. As is well known, the doctor who eventually performed the operation was prosecuted at the Old Bailey and acquitted.

Perhaps the most interesting case in which Miss Wyles was professionally concerned—it certainly received the widest publicity at the time—was that of Miss Irene Savage in 1928, since it led to serious charges being brought against the police of employing 'third-degree' methods in the interrogation of

* Lilian Wyles. *A Woman at Scotland Yard* (1952).

persons in custody and also of giving perjured evidence. Miss Savage, a factory employee, had gone for a walk with an ex-M.P., Sir Leo Chiozza Money, in Hyde Park, when they had been arrested by two police constables and charged with an unpleasant offence. At the subsequent police court hearing they were discharged, while at the same time it was suggested on behalf of Sir Leo Money that the two police constables had given false evidence.

The Commissioner of Police instructed Chief Inspector Alfred Collins to make a full inquiry into the alleged perjury and it was the nature of the examination of Miss Savage by the Chief Inspector and his assistant, Detective-Sergeant Clarke, which led to the 'third degree' accusation. Miss Wyles accompanied Irene Savage to Scotland Yard, but was not present when she was questioned.

The matter was raised in Parliament and a judicial inquiry ordered. At this investigation the police were completely exonerated of the charges against them, although the Chief Inspector was shown to be over-zealous. Indeed he realised that, in deliberately excluding a woman police officer from the questioning of Miss Savage, he had made a foolish mistake.

If similar circumstances were to arise today, it is safe to assume that a woman member of the force would invariably be present. The women police have indeed justified their existence.

6. The I.R.A. Coventry Explosion

AMONG the laws, which come up for renewal annually by Parliament and which invariably provoke M.P.s to lively discussion is the Prevention of Violence (Temporary Provisions) Act. This measure was originally passed in July, 1939, to enable the authorities to deal effectively with the terrorist campaign of the Irish Republican Army, which had been launched in England earlier the same year. Besides giving the police power to arrest persons suspected of complicity in terrorist acts without warrant and to detain them for five days, the Act authorises the Home Secretary to expel suspected residents in England from the country and to prohibit other suspects from entering it. In 1953, fourteen years after the Act first became law, nine expulsion orders and forty-eight prohibition orders were still in force.*

It was the declared aim of the I.R.A. to unite Northern Ireland, which remains an integral part of the United Kingdom, by force with the south. On January 12, 1939, six prominent Republicans, including Mr. Sean Russell, the I.R.A. Chief of Staff, sent a joint letter to the Prime Ministers of Great Britain and Northern Ireland, Hitler, Mussolini and other notabilities, demanding the withdrawal of British troops from Ireland within four days, in default of which they threatened to take 'appropriate action without further notice'.

The threat was not an idle one. Four days later a series of widely distributed bomb explosions took place, damaging electricity plants and gas mains in different parts of the country. One man was killed in Manchester and two others injured.

The campaign continued for the next fifteen months, bombs being placed in public lavatories, telephone kiosks, pillar-boxes, railway cloak-rooms and elsewhere, with resultant loss of life and damage to property. In March, 1939, for instance, an unsuccessful attempt was made to blow up Hammersmith Bridge. In June a bomb planted in Piccadilly Circus deprived a passer-by of an eye. In the following month an explosion in the left luggage office at King's Cross station killed a traveller on holiday from Edinburgh, and severely injured his wife and fourteen other persons. A similar explosion at Victoria station on the same day wounded five of the railway staff.

By July, 1939, 127 outrages had taken place, 66 members of the I.R.A. had been convicted and large quantities of explosives seized by the police. In introducing the Prevention of Violence Bill, the Home Secretary, then Sir Samuel Hoare, gave the House of Commons these particulars and also stated that the terrorist campaign was being "closely watched and actively stimulated by foreign organisations".

---

* This is an improvement on 1952, when the numbers were 117 expulsion orders and 57 prohibition orders.

The work of the authorities in tracking down the terrorists was considerably facilitated by the carelessness which the latter displayed in the custody of secret documents. In one instance a coded message and the cypher key were left in the same drawer. Amongst the documents thus captured at an early stage in the campaign was the so-called 'S' Plan, which contained detailed instructions on the sabotage of public services and key industries. As the Home Secretary told the House of Commons at the time, it was not the kind of irresponsible melodramatic document that one sometimes discovers in these searches. "It is a very carefully worked out staff plan, the kind of plan that might be worked out by a General Staff, setting out in detail the way in which an extensive campaign of sabotage could be successfully carried out against this country." It was thought to have been the work of Sean Russell, who had in the meantime gone to the United States to raise further funds.

On August 25, 1939, occurred the most serious outrage in the whole campaign. A bomb exploded in a crowded street in Coventry, killing five people, injuring sixty others, all innocent passers-by, and causing extensive damage to the surroundings. As a result five persons were arrested and charged with murder. Their trial, which took place at Birmingham Assizes before Mr. Justice Singleton, forms the subject of an interesting volume in the Notable British Trials Series.* This work, which has been admirably edited by Dr. Letitia Fairfield, also contains much interesting new material on I.R.A. activities generally, including practically the whole text of the 'S' Plan, here reproduced for the first time from the files of Scotland Yard.

The central figure in the trial was a young man of the labouring class, who called himself James Richards and had been sent to Coventry as an 'operating officer' of the I.R.A. He lodged with a fellow Irishman named Hewitt, his wife and mother-in-law, who was called Mrs. O'Hara. It was established in court that Richards, whose real name was McCormac, had the principal hand in the manufacture of the bomb. He was

* *Trial of Peter Barnes and Others.* Edited by Letitia Fairfield (1953).

I.R.A. Bomb Outrage at Coventry

assisted by a 'strange man', whose identity none of the accused was either able or willing to disclose, and who actually placed the bomb in the carrier of a bicycle, which he left standing against the street kerb. This mysterious individual was unfortunately never caught, although the authorities later became aware of his name. But another man, Peter Barnes, who was proved to have supplied the explosives used in the bomb, was arraigned along with Richards, the two Hewitts and Mrs. O'Hara.

In framing a charge of murder, the prosecution invoked what is known as the doctrine of common purpose. This is to the effect that when two or more persons conspire together to commit a dangerous felony which results in the death of another, all the persons in the conspiracy are guilty of murder, even if they did not do the actual killing. English criminal trials furnish many examples of the application of this doctrine, of which the most recent is the case of Derek Bentley.

In this trial Barnes and Richards were convicted and sentenced to death. From the dock Richards made a short speech in the highest tradition of Irish martyrology claiming that what he had done was "for a just cause". Both he and Barnes were subsequently executed. The other three were acquitted, since the prosecution could not prove to the satisfaction of the jury that they knew what had been going on.

The Coventry bomb explosion marked the peak of the terror campaign. Other incidents occurred, but they were all of a minor character. The I.R.A. leaders were divided on the wisdom of Eire's official policy of neutrality in the war, and the movement against Britain gradually petered out. Its epitaph may be read in the subsequent fate of Sean Russell.

The I.R.A. Chief of Staff returned from America to Europe in the spring of 1940, landing in Genoa and continuing his journey under Nazi guidance by road to Berlin. Here he had several secret meetings with Hitler's Foreign Minister, Ribbentrop, whom he is said to have convinced of the necessity for Germany to co-operate with the I.R.A. as part of 'Operation Sea Lion', the Nazi plan for the invasion of Britain. To this end, several months later, Russell was put on board a German submarine, whose commander had instructions to land him on the west coast of Ireland.

He never reached his destination. He was suffering from a duodenal ulcer which ruptured, and he died on the voyage. He was buried at sea, about a hundred miles from the country which, in Dr. Fairfield's words, "he served so devotedly and so unwisely".

7. THE STRANGE DISAPPEARANCE OF MR. BATHURST

MR. DONALD MACLEAN and Mr. Guy Burgess are not the first British diplomats to have been reported missing. Their recent disappearance recalls the curious story of another Foreign Office official, Mr. Benjamin Bathurst, who vanished mysteriously on his way from Vienna to London during the Napoleonic Wars and was never heard of again.

The prevailing idea at the time was that Bathurst was assassinated on Napoleon's orders on account of the important despatches he was carrying, and this view is the generally accepted one. Personally I do not believe it, and think there is a more convincing explanation.

Benjamin Bathurst was a younger son of Henry Bathurst, Bishop of Norwich, and was related to Earl Bathurst, who held various Cabinet posts in the early years of the last century. He was born in 1784, and through his kinsman's influence he entered the diplomatic service after leaving Oxford. Shortly after this he married a daughter of Sir John Call, a Cornish baronet, and had two children by her.

In 1809, while serving as Secretary of Legation in Stockholm, Bathurst was instructed to proceed as Envoy to the Court of Vienna. The selection of a young man of twenty-five for such an important appointment was doubtless due to the action of his noble relative, Lord Bathurst, who had recently become Foreign Minister. At the same time the new Envoy seems to have been generally regarded as a young man of exceptional ability.

Unfortunately Mr. Bathurst was not to have much opportunity of showing his gifts. He had barely reached his destination, when Austria was severely defeated by Napoleon and forced to conclude a humiliating peace. Under its terms she was debarred from all intercourse with England; the British Embassy in Vienna was consequently closed down and the staff prepared to return home. Because of the turn the fighting had taken in Europe, they had to travel through Prussia to Hamburg and thence by sea to England.

Bathurst set out in his private post-chaise, accompanied by his valet, Ilbert, and the Embassy messenger, whose name was Krause. They broke their journey for a few days in Berlin and then pushed on in the direction of the Baltic coast. It later transpired that Bathurst thought he might be waylaid on the route, and for this reason had provided himself with a passport in the name of a merchant called Koch, apparently bound for Hamburg, under which name, in fact, he travelled.

On the afternoon of November 25, 1809, the party reached a little town called Perleberg, where they stopped for refreshment at the local post-house. That Bathurst was already in fear for his life is evidenced by the fact that, as soon as he arrived, he went to call on the town major, Captain von Klitzing, who was, of course, a Prussian officer, and appealed to him for protection. The town major, who appears to have been aware of the traveller's identity, returned with him to the post-house, escorted by two troopers, who were told to remain on guard until Bathurst and his two companions were ready to leave.

The postmaster, whose duty it was to provide travellers with overnight accommodation when they required it, was struck by the young man's fine clothes. He wore a fur coat with a white border, underneath which could be seen a pair of dark-coloured trousers. He asked the postmaster for rooms for himself and the messenger, but was told that all the rooms had been taken. The postmaster recommended a good inn. However, Bathurst replied that he had unpacked all his papers and that he could not leave the post-house as he had a lot of writing to do. The table at which he sat was seen to be covered with papers.

A little later the postmaster returned to say that he had been able to fix up accommodation after all, provided that he and the messenger did not object to sharing a room. He was still sitting at the table writing. "That is good," he said. "I have still to write." He then ordered some supper and the postmaster left him to go back to his own work.

During the next hour or so Bathurst changed his mind about staying the night. He ordered his carriage, then countermanded the order; in fact he did this several times. Finally, he made up his mind to leave and dismissed the two troopers who had been on guard. One of the maids in the post-house subsequently reported that he also went into the kitchen, where he burnt some of his papers in the stove. A little later he was seen in the street supervising the loading of his luggage on to the carriage. But when the time came for his departure, he could not be found anywhere. Search was made all over the town, but there was no trace of the missing man. When the matter was reported to the town major, he put Ilbert and Krause under arrest pending inquiries, but it seemed that they knew nothing and they were soon released.

In the course of the proceedings against these two men Bathurst's fur coat was missed. Suspicion fell upon a maid employed by the head groom in charge of the post-house stables. The town major turned this matter over to the civil authorities and the magistrates, who, perhaps somewhat old-fashioned in their methods of criminal investigation, offered the girl the choice between a reward of five crowns for showing them where the coat was hidden, or of being whipped for withholding the information. Recourse was had to the latter alternative, as a result of which the coat was found in the groom's wood-shed and his son was sent to prison for stealing it. But it transpired that the thief had not taken it from Bathurst's body, but had simply found it lying about after the traveller's disappearance and had misappropriated it.

A fortnight later a discovery of more importance was made. Two women who were gathering sticks in a wood near the town found a pair of trousers turned inside out, in one of the pockets of which was a paper with writing on it. The women hastened back to the town and handed over their find to the authorities. It was then established beyond all doubt that the trousers were those which Bathurst had been wearing on the day of his disappearance. The paper formed part of a letter to his wife, in which he wrote of the dangers by which he was beset, and expressed a hope that she would not re-marry, should the worst befall him. Further search was thereupon ordered to be made, but no further traces of the missing diplomat were discovered.

The Prussian Government evinced the deepest regret on learning what had happened, and offered a large reward for the recovery of the body. But nobody ever came forward. The French authorities, on the other hand, gave it out that Bathurst's mind was deranged. "It is the custom of the British Cabinet," wrote Napoleon's organ *Le Moniteur*, "to entrust diplomatic missions to persons whom the whole nation knows are half fools. It is only the English diplomatic service which contains crazy people." Meanwhile the young man's family at home soon gave up all hope that he was alive. There were rumours that he had committed suicide, but these were discounted by seeming absence of any motive. "He has lost no money at play," wrote Lord Bathurst to the young man's mother, "nor has he in any way misconducted himself."

The young man had left a wife and children, and Mrs. Bathurst was determined to probe the mystery. She managed to obtain a safe-conduct from Napoleon through a neutral source and in the following year set off for Prussia by way of Sweden. Her visit was unproductive, apart from the fact that she received a message from Napoleon when she was in Berlin to the effect that on his word of honour he knew nothing of her husband's disappearance. But she could not bring herself to accept this assurance: on the contrary she was always of the belief that he had been done away with by Napoleon's orders for the sake of the documents he was supposed to be carrying. However, the fact remains that all the diplomatic documents of importance were in the charge of the messenger Krause, and these were subsequently accounted for.

More than forty years elapsed before any fresh clues were discovered. In 1852 some workmen were pulling down an old house in the neighbourhood, and they came upon a skeleton of a man inside. The absence of clothes, and the fact that the skull had been fractured by a hatchet, suggested that the remains were those of Mr. Bathurst and that he had been put to death in this manner.

By a curious coincidence, a few months later the missing man's sister, Mrs. Thislethwayte, visited Perleberg. She examined the skull and said she did not think it belonged to her brother. But this must not be accepted as conclusive evidence against such a supposition, particularly when it is remembered that Goethe failed to recognise the skull of Schiller, his intimate friend, when it was shown to him. On the contrary, the belief that the skeleton was Bathurst's received support from the fact that the house had formerly been inhabited by a waiter named Martins who worked at an inn near the post-house. This waiter had two daughters and, when they got married, he was able to give them a dowry of over £150 each, a large sum for a waiter at an inn in an obscure Prussian town. At the time of Bathurst's disappearance the diplomat was known to have a large sum of money with him, which was never recovered.

It seems certain that Bathurst was murdered either in the post-house at Perleberg or in a house near-by. The question remains, by whom? Not by Napoleon's agents, for the reason already given. Nor by the Prussian Government, since neither King Frederick William of Prussia nor his Ministers had any conceivable pretext for interfering with him. There is a more likely explanation than either of these.

It will be remembered that Bathurst had stayed a few days in Berlin on his fatal journey. At this time Prussia was firmly under the Napoleonic yoke, but there existed a secret military association, with headquarters in Berlin, which formed the core of 'resistance' to French occupation. It is fairly certain that Bathurst had been in touch with this underground movement through secret service channels. It seems that Bathurst talked indiscreetly in Berlin—he had to be warned of the danger of his conduct during a visit to the theatre—and it is very likely that the Prussian underground leaders considered that he might betray them by his conduct and for that reason arranged with the town major at Perleberg to take drastic measures to render him harmless.

Certain it is that as he grew older any reference to Mr. Bathurst's disappearance seemed to be most distasteful to Captain von Klitzing. If the subject were mentioned, the town major would never discuss it, but would endeavour to turn the conversation into other channels. His friends never doubted that he knew more about the affair than anyone and was under a solemn oath of obligation never to divulge the truth.

8. WHY DO THEY CONFESS?

BETWEEN the two world wars I paid a visit to Moscow. It was just after the trial of the British engineers from the Metropolitan-Vickers works, who had been accused of sabotaging the Five Year Plan. After several months in detention, they had appeared in court and some of them had made astonishing confessions.

I remember being taken past the grim-looking Lubianka Prison, or rather hurried past it, as my guide obviously thought it was not a place to linger near. I wondered, as I gazed at its grey walls, what processes went on behind them to obtain such abject admissions of guilt.

Other trials took place on a larger scale after I left Russia. In 1936 there were the trials of the 'Old Guard' Bolsheviks, men like Zinoviev, Radek and Bukharin, who had been Lenin's comrades-in-arms. A similar purge occurred a year later with the mass indictment of Marshal Tukachevsky and other Red Army leaders.

These trials followed an identical pattern. The defendants vied with each other in their efforts of self-accusation. Men who had filled high and prominent positions in the State confessed to the most heinous treachery against the Soviet fatherland. In spite of their pleas for mercy they were convicted and subsequently 'liquidated'.

Western observers were bewildered by these extraordinary

confessions and sought in vain to explain them. My parliamentary colleague, Brigadier Fitzroy Maclean, M.P., who was present at the trial of Bukharin and others, supposed that torture had been employed. By some it was believed that drugs had been used. But the prisoners always seemed in good health and, although in many instances they repeated their stories like actors playing their parts, on the whole they appeared self-possessed. How could one account for it?

In 1940 Mr. Arthur Koestler published his famous book *Darkness at Noon*, which contained a brilliant but hypothetical explanation. His view was that a Communist on trial would confess to any crime against the State because he would realise that his confession, even though substantially false, was the only way left to him in which he could advance the cause of Communism. In other words, to abandon belief in Communism after a lifetime as a revolutionary was psychologically impossible. Thus with the broken men of the opposition recantation had become a kind of ritual habit and accepted routine.

But this explanation seems to be but partly true. It can only apply to those who believe in the Marxist gospel; for it implies basic solidarity with the social régime which has become identified with the rule of Stalin. It cannot have applied to the Metropolitan-Vickers engineers, nor to other non-Communists, such as Cardinal Mindszenty or the sixteen Polish leaders who were carried off to Moscow in 1945 and charged with sabotaging the Soviet war effort in Poland.

Fifteen of these Poles pleaded guilty at their trial. The sixteenth, Mr. Z. Stypulkowski, unlike his companions, refused to confess in prison. On the contrary, he insisted on pleading not guilty in court. What is even more surprising, he has survived to tell the remarkable tale of his experience in the Lubianka Prison.* He is almost the only living witness who, although publicly accused before the Supreme Court of the U.S.S.R., has been able to put on record the truth about the Soviet methods of breaking down their victims both physically and morally.

* Z. Stypulkowsky. *Invitation to Moscow* (1951).

A barrister and former officer in the Polish Army, Mr. Stypulkowski was taken prisoner in 1939, first by the Reds and later by the Germans. He later found his way back to Warsaw, where he started underground activities and became one of the leaders of the Resistance movement, and in 1944 took part in the abortive Warsaw rising. Early in the following year, together with fifteen other Polish underground leaders, he was invited to Moscow to meet Marshal Zhukov, Commander-in-Chief of the Soviet Forces, to discuss outstanding problems concerning Soviet-occupied Polish territory. Instead of being received as a delegate, he was kidnapped and thrown into the Lubianka. There the N.K.V.D., the dreaded secret police, did their best to make him confess to having plotted against the Soviet Union.

He was not subjected to torture, but he was the victim of the most intensive third-degree methods, in which it was sought to wear down his resistance by regulated discomfort. He was dragged from bed on seventy nights out of seventy-one, and suffered 141 protracted interrogations. By sheer force of will-power he dominated his interrogator. His harrowing experiences enabled him to explain the submission of his fifteen colleagues, who were in reality equally guiltless.

The prisoner is confined in a cell under constant surveillance of a guard, under the harsh glare of a strong electric light, the prey of ceaseless anxiety and fears. In these surroundings and after nights of repeated questioning his sense of values becomes blurred and he is inclined to accept the idea put into his mind by the interrogator. This is that his paramount duty is to recover his freedom. The price does not seem unduly high—just his signature on a deposition acknowledging his traitorous acts against the Soviet.

Meanwhile his faculties have become diminished and his reasoning powers corrupted. He confuses true facts with those suggested to him by his interrogator. Finally, in his determination to confess everything he talks about things which have never happened. He tries to remember something he never did, he tries to remember some action he never committed, just to prove conclusively that he does not intend to conceal anything. After the fortieth interrogation or so the prisoner's deposition usually begins, "Yes, I didn't state the truth until now. Now I will tell everything openly. . . ."

By this time the prisoner is a nervous wreck. Having stated what is required of him he is then put on a better diet and deliberately fattened up for the public trial. Any attempt on his part to deviate from his story in court is countered by the prosecutor reminding him sharply of the details of his confession.

Mr. Stypulkowsky was lucky. True, he was convicted, but he received the extremely light sentence of four months, most of which he had already spent in gaol, so that he was released almost immediately. While the Soviet authorities were anxious to discredit the Polish Resistance movement at that time, they also desired to keep up the appearance of harmony with the West. With fifteen pleas of guilty they could afford a few acquittals to please their allies.

The story which Mr. Stypulkowski has to tell makes fascinating reading. It is the most convincing account of Communist technique in treason trials which I have read. The reason for this is clear. It affords the most likely explanation of just why political prisoners under the Soviet confess to crimes they have never committed. I believe it to be the true one.

9. CRIME IN THE UNITED STATES

I VISITED the United States as the last war was drawing to an end: and I went to see Mr. J. Edgar Hoover, the director of the Federal Bureau of Investigation, at his offices in Washington. Mr. Hoover talked to me at length about the F.B.I.'s record as a law enforcement agency during the inter-war years—the suppression of kidnapping and other 'rackets', the warfare between rival groups of gangsters in American cities, and so on. Then he discussed the prospects of post-war law enforcement in the United States.

It was a gloomy picture that he drew. He envisaged a resurgence of gangsterism on a vast scale, stimulated by ex-servicemen returning from overseas who would be unable to re-settle themselves in civilian life. Then he made a prediction. The post-war American criminal, he said, would employ methods much subtler than the violence so popular with inter-war criminals. The gun would only be used as a last resort.

Events have proved Mr. Hoover right. The new aristocrats of the American criminal world today are not the rough, ape-like killers of the 'twenties. They have been replaced by smooth-spoken and impeccably tailored individuals—'hoodlums', to give them their vernacular name. "We're business men," they protest in answer to any embarrassing inquiry about their activities. "We live quietly, pay our income taxes, and give the public only what it wants."

What certain sections of the American public want are narcotics, black-market commodities, prostitutes and extensive gambling facilities. It is the aim of the hoodlums to provide these services—at a price—and to bribe the authorities to turn a blind eye to their existence.

These facts have emerged from the inquiries being instituted by the U.S. Senate Crime Investigating Committee under the chairmanship of Senator Estes Kefauver, forty-eight-year-old Democrat from Tennessee, and one-time candidate for his party's nomination for President. The committee's findings, which were widely publicised and televised in America, have since been published in this country.* They make startling and unsavoury reading.

According to Senator Kefauver, a nation-wide crime syndicate exists in the United States. It is a loosely organised but cohesive coalition of autonomous crime organisations, which work together for mutual profit. Their activities are controlled by a cynical partnership of hoodlums, venal politicians and conscienceless business and professional men, including accountants and lawyers. Behind them Mr. Kefauver even sees the hand of the Mafia—though it must be admitted there is no clear evidence of the operation of this subterranean Italian organisation in the United States.

However, despite the fact that some of their conclusions

* *Crime in America.* By Estes Kefauver (1951).

may be mistaken, the Kefauver Committee have revealed that, now the great days of Prohibition are over, organised gambling, which is illegal in every State except Nevada, has replaced bootlegging as the gangsters' most profitable source of income. Between 17 and 25 million dollars are spent annually on this 'racket' in the U.S.A. This and other forms of organised crime go hand in hand with the most shameless political corruption —as is evident from the examination of a variety of witnesses before the Senate Committee.

Here is an extract from the testimony of Mr. Thomas J. Cawley, who is described as the undisputed gambling king of the town of La Salle, in Illinois. Cawley admitted in effect that he bribed the authorities to ignore his business by contributing to their election expenses.

CHAIRMAN: Do you know Mike Welter?
WITNESS: Yes, sir. . . . He was Sheriff three times.
CHAIRMAN: How much did you contribute to his campaign?
WITNESS: Five hundred dollars.
CHAIRMAN: Mike Welter knew what business you were in?
WITNESS: I wouldn't know whether he would or not.
CHAIRMAN: Why?
WITNESS: I never asked him.
CHAIRMAN: What we want to get at is this. How can you run down there without the Sheriff knowing something about it and doing something about it? It is generally known, is it not, that you operate these places?
WITNESS: That is right. I was born and raised there. I had a good friend, the Mayor of the town, and he wouldn't let none of them politicians come into our city.
CHAIRMAN: He would not let the Sheriff come in?
WITNESS: That is right.
CHAIRMAN: Do the people like it, you think?
WITNESS: I think they do—ninety per cent of them.

Walter Clark, a county Sheriff in Florida, near Miami, was asked why he violated his oath by letting gamblers operate openly in his county. "I was elected on a liberal ticket, and the people want it and they enjoy it," was the brazen reply. "I let them have what they want for the tourists down here." Pressed to define what he meant by 'liberal', this astonishing Sheriff said, "Well, I am not going around snooping in private businesses and homes."

Another aspect of the American crime world has been the extent to which various Federal agencies, particularly the Internal Revenue Bureau, have been in league with the law-breakers and have even collected tribute from them.

Laxity in scrutinising income-tax returns, submitted by known gamblers and others, reached such scandalous proportions that President Truman was obliged to take drastic action. An Assistant Attorney-General and several hundred revenue officials have been dismissed; prosecutions are pending against some of these officials on charges of receiving bribes. One such official even enclosed a Government-franked envelope in his letter demanding money from a woman who ran a house of prostitution. He wrote, "I am most grateful for everything you did for me, but I am wondering if you could let me have another 75 dollars or 100 dollars to complete my repair and painting job." Then he added, "Please use the enclosed envelope, which requires no postage, at your earliest convenience." It is this alliance between organised crime and corrupt politicians that is emphasised by the Kefauver Report.

10. How Safe are the Mails?

UNTIL the latter part of the eighteenth century, when the mails were carried by post-boys on horseback, mail robberies in this country were frequent. Nor were large-scale thefts uncommon in later days, before the building of the railways, when the mail went by stage coach. In those days the carriage of mails was so unsafe that the Post Office advised the public who wished to send banknotes through the post to cut them in half and send the halves at different times.

But for well over a century we have prided ourselves in Britain on the comparative security of the mails. When we post a letter, we are accustomed to feel that it will be delivered safely and that there will be no interference with its contents in transit. Registered packages have always enjoyed an additional protection by reason of the particular care with which they are handled, and the chance of such packages falling into wrong hands has been regarded, at any rate until quite recently, as very remote.

It would be an exaggeration to say that public confidence in the postal service has been seriously undermined by recent thefts of mail bags. But it cannot be denied that there is considerable anxiety on the part of the public at the incidents which have happened lately and which have received wide publicity in certain sections of the Press. Even the Queen's personal mail has not been immune from unauthorised interference. These incidents have led to an understandable demand in Parliament for the improvement of security measures in the Post Office.

The most serious mail robbery in recent times—indeed one of the worst in the whole history of the British Post Office—occurred in London in the early hours of the morning of May 21, 1952. Seven masked men attacked the driver of a mail van, and two Post Office officials with him, on their way from Paddington station to the City. The bags in the van contained Treasury notes which had been sent by provincial banks to their head offices in London.

Two of the men in the van were badly injured and left lying unconscious on the pavement. Meanwhile the robbers succeeded in getting away with notes to the value of £200,000. None of the robbers has been caught. Neither has any of the money been recovered. It was subsequently found that the alarm bell, which is fitted to every Post Office van, had been tampered with.

Since the liability of the Post Office for loss is limited to £5 for each registered package and there were ninety packages stolen on this occasion, the monetary responsibility of the Post Office to the banks concerned amounted to only £450. Since the packages were also insured, the remaining loss was borne by the underwriters.

This spectacular robbery led the Government to appoint a committee of experts to examine the whole problem of safeguarding the mails, in consultation with the police and other authorities, and to make recommendations. In the course of a recent debate on the subject in the House of Lords, the Postmaster-General, Earl De La Warr, gave some information on the nature of some of the additional precautions which have been taken. They include better liaison with the railways and the police, the use of radio warnings, the provision of many more locked cages in corridor trains, the doubling of the Post Office investigation branch and changes in the routes followed by high-value package services. One of the routes changed for security reasons was the Redhill to East Grinstead route, the scene of a recent highway robbery. When this robbery took place, there were, consequently, no packets of high value in the van which was held up, and the thieves were disappointed. At the same time the Postmaster-General made it clear that he could not promise immunity to the mails. "With the number of criminal gangs and thugs going about today," he said, "it is inevitable that we are going to have more attacks. And one thing we can be sure of—they are going to think up new methods and new plans. We shall do our best to repel those attacks by improving our precautions."

No interested observer can doubt that there is room for improvement. The other day a newspaperman wandered all over the London G.P.O. at Mount Pleasant without being challenged. I have myself seen bags of mail lying unattended at night in dingy and ill-lit railway stations, and I have also seen Post Office vans standing unattended in the street. It was due to the momentary absence of the driver and guard that a van was robbed of £4,700 at Walthamstow in January, 1954. In the case of the even more recent theft of precious stones and other valuables while in transit to a well-known firm of jewellers in Regent Street, the driver of the van has been charged with complicity in the robbery.

On the question of internal security, it should be remembered that there are 160,000 men and women on the postal staff. Nearly as many again are employed temporarily during the Christmas season. In such a large organisation Lord De La Warr has admitted that there are bound to be weak links. But on the whole the Minister is satisfied with the way in which his staff have responded to the present challenge and are doing a difficult job under trying conditions.

Some further facts and figures may be borne in mind. In spite of recent incidents, the number of mailbag robberies has decreased since the end of the last war. Out of approximately 350 million bags carried by the Post Office every year, 1,200, or three per million, were lost in 1947. The figure has now dropped to 720, or two per million. During the same period losses of registered letters have fallen from 11,000 to 7,000 and of registered parcels from 6,900 to 2,300. Nor is it true to say, as I sometimes hear, that mail thieves are never brought to justice. In 1953 457 people were caught for direct robbery of the mail.

Finally, when set against the fact that money and valuables in the sum of well over £2,000,000,000 are carried annually by registered post in this country, the losses which have actually occurred are not so alarming as may at first appear. That does not mean that there is any excuse for complacency. The Post Office must push ahead with its precautions and spare no efforts to reduce still further the number of mail losses.

At the same time, we must not forget that when we drop a letter into the pillar-box at the end of the street or hand a registered package over the counter at our local post office, the odds are 500,000 to one against these articles failing to reach their destination. Can any other country in the world boast as fine a record as this? I doubt it.

GEORGE CHAPMAN

View of the Yard with Drums used by Haigh

IV. THE ENIGMA OF THE MULTIPLE MURDERER

IV. THE ENIGMA OF THE MULTIPLE MURDERER

1. MULTIPLE MURDERS IN HISTORY

SENSATIONAL as it was, the trial of John Reginald Halliday Christie, which was concluded at the Central Criminal Court in London in June, 1953, is by no means unique. There have been similar cases in various countries, where the evidence has shown that the accused committed, not merely one murder, but a series of murders. Sometimes this seems to have taken the form of killing for killing's sake, with no other motive; sometimes it has been connected with some form of sexual perversion or lust for power. More often, however, the multiple murderer has killed because there is no other way of getting hold of his victim's money and possessions.

Most people are familiar with the story of Bluebeard, which has found its way into the common stock of European folklore. Though generally related as a fairy-tale for children, it has some foundation in fact. The original Bluebeard is believed to have been a Breton chief of the sixth century named Comorre, who killed seven of his wives and hid them in a locked room. It was the disobedience of his eighth spouse, who succeeded in entering the forbidden chamber, which led to the discovery of her husband's guilty secret and incidentally her own timely rescue.

In Bluebeard's case the motive was probably greed. In our own times it had its counterpart in the activities of the notorious Henri Landru, who was guillotined for the murder of ten women and the child of one of them in France shortly after the First World War.

Then there is the sex murder. The classic example of sadism in its extreme form, involving the killing of large numbers of boys and girls, is Gilles de Rais, the Marshal of France, who fought beside Joan of Arc at Orleans in the fifteenth century. Indeed, it is said that his association with the 'Maid of Orleans' was responsible for his becoming mentally unbalanced. His servants kidnapped child victims, generally boys, on his behalf, and these he tortured and murdered. He was eventually brought to justice before an ecclesiastical court, condemned to death and subsequently hanged. At his trial the total number of his victims was stated to be 140, and these he confessed to; but he may well have killed more. He remains probably the most terrible sadistic maniac in the annals of crime.

A comparable case, though on a smaller scale, was that of Fritz Haarmann, a 'black market' butcher in Hanover, who was executed in 1924 for the murder of twenty-four youths. Haarmann was also a homosexual, who used to entice his victims to his house and then slaughter them in unspeakable circumstances.

Other victims of the sadistic mass-murderer have been women. Such cases are fortunately not numerous, but they have occurred from time to time in England, among other countries. For instance, there was the mysterious criminal known as 'Jack the Ripper', whose victims were invariably prostitutes. There was that other lustful product of the late-Victorian age, Dr. Thomas Neil Cream, who killed several women of easy virtue, partly for the pleasure it gave him and partly from a sense of power mania.

A wholly sadistic murderer, on the other hand, was Neville Heath, who murdered two women within a few weeks of each other in 1946, and might have done away with more if he had not been arrested immediately after the second crime. The horrible condition of both his victims' bodies suggested plain blood lust. Before killing his first victim he had tied her up and cruelly lashed her with a metal-tipped riding whip. Seventeen weals were found on her body after death.

Killing for killing's sake, without hope of material gain, is mercifully rare, but it is not confined exclusively to the male sex. Examples of such female monsters in the last century are Jegado in France and Van der Leyden in Holland. Both were nurses, short and ugly, whose position enabled them to gratify their taste for cruelty, with which a craving for power was also doubtless associated. Jegado was guilty of twenty-six poisonings and eight attempted poisonings between 1833 and 1851. "Wherever I go people die," she said. Van der Leyden killed twenty-seven by poison and attempted to do away with 122 others in a similar manner between the years 1869 and 1885. Her victims included her own father and mother and three of her children. To a man whom she saw mourning the loss of a relative who had died as the result of her nursing, she said, "It will be your turn next month". It was.

Poisoning has always been a favourite method of wholesale murderers, partly because of the difficulty of detection and partly, in the case of sadistic crimes, because the victims frequently have died in great pain. Prince among English poisoners was the infamous William Palmer, who came from Rugeley in Staffordshire, where he practised medicine. He was executed in 1856 for an appalling series of murders. His victims included four of his legitimate and three of his illegitimate children, and three boon companions, as well as his wife, mother-in-law, uncle and mother. His motive was mainly greed.

Another English poisoner, who flourished in the nineteenth century and also achieved considerable success as a painter and art critic, was Thomas Griffiths Wainewright. He was eventually tried at the Old Bailey on a charge of forging a trust deed and sentenced to transportation. While in Newgate gaol he was recognised by the actor Macready, who was being shown over the prison in company with Charles Dickens. When he was reproached by one of them for poisoning his sister-in-law, Wainewright is said to have shrugged his shoulders and declared, "Yes, it was a dreadful thing to do, but she had very thick ankles".

Criminal killing on an extended scale has been by no means unknown in the present century. I have already referred to the cases of Landru, Haarmann and Heath. As recently as 1931 Silvester Matuska admitted to having murdered no fewer than twenty-seven people in railway crashes which he engineered on the Continent of Europe.

Bloch, of Chicago, killed twenty-six. Marcel Petiot, who

was guillotined in 1946, was believed to have slaughtered no less than sixty-one victims.

After careful consideration of those cases which have come to trial during the last fifty years, I have selected five as worthy of fuller treatment because of their particular interest and importance.

Landru, the modern French Bluebeard, is an obvious choice. So is the case of Martha Beck and Raymond Fernandez, the amazing 'Lonely Hearts' murderers in America. The remaining three cases have occurred in England—Chapman, the poisoner, who was almost certainly identical with 'Jack the Ripper'; George Joseph Smith, the 'Brides-in-the-Bath' murderer; and finally John George Haigh, who dissolved the bodies of his victims in sulphuric acid.

2. POISONER—AND RIPPER?

ONE of the most remarkable examples of wholesale murder was revealed early in the present century when a thirty-six-year-old Pole, who passed under the name of George Chapman, stood in the dock at the Old Bailey.

The accused, whose real name was Severin Klosowski, was brought up in a Polish village where his father was a carpenter, and for a time followed the profession of *feldscher*, or barber-surgeon, in his native country. When he was about twenty-four years of age, Klosowski migrated to London, where he found work as a hairdresser's assistant in Whitechapel. Soon after his arrival he married a Polish woman named Lucy Baderski, and together they went to America, where they stayed for several years. Here they separated, because of the husband's fondness for other women, and she returned to England alone. He followed a little later, turning up again in the East End. Here he began living with a young woman named Annie Chapman, thenceforth adopting her surname and calling himself George Chapman, by which name he was afterwards generally known. Fortunately for herself, she, too, left him when they had been together for only a short period.

Chapman now took up with a woman named Mrs. Mary Spink, the wife of a porter on the Great Eastern Railway who had left her on account of her intemperate habits. They posed as man and wife, and, as Mrs. Spink had a little money of her own, Chapman gave up his job as a hairdresser's assistant and with her financial help opened a barber's shop in Hastings. Among the customers was a chemist named Davidson, from whom he bought an ounce of tartar-emetic. This purchase was entered by the chemist in his poisons book, as required by law, and he obtained Chapman's signature to it. The main ingredient of this poison is antimony, a substance almost tasteless to the palate and colourless to the eye. Two grains have been known to be fatal to the human body; Chapman's purchase contained about 150.

In 1897 Chapman and his supposed wife returned to London, where he became the lessee of a public-house in Finsbury. Hitherto a healthy woman in spite of frequent drinking bouts, Mrs. Spink now became ill; she was confined to bed suffering from severe vomiting attacks and distressing abdominal pains. She slowly became weaker and eventually died in acute agony on Christmas Day.

Not long afterwards Chapman advertised for a barmaid, and there were numerous applicants for the position. Eventually his choice fell on a strong, healthy young woman named Bessie Taylor, a farmer's daughter. She was engaged, and, like the late Mrs. Spink, soon became known as Mrs. Chapman. By this time Chapman had moved to the Monument Tavern, in the Borough, on the south side of the Thames. In due course she became ill, displaying similar symptoms to those of her predecessor, gradually becoming thinner, and eventually on February 13, 1901, dying in great pain.

Dr. Stoker, the medical practitioner who attended her during her illness, was puzzled by her case. On the death certificate he ascribed her passing to "exhaustion from vomiting and diarrhoea". She was buried near her native village in Cheshire.

Six months later Chapman chanced to see an advertisement in which another young woman sought a position as barmaid.

The name of this advertiser was Maud Marsh, and it was by reason of her death that Chapman was ultimately arrested and brought to justice. Maud Marsh was engaged. To satisfy her parents, who were naturally interested in their daughter's future, he told them that he was a widower and that there was a family living in the house.

Shortly afterwards it was given out that they had married. Early in 1902 they removed to the Crown Tavern in the Borough, the Monument having been burned down. In fact, Chapman almost certainly set fire to the place himself in order to get the insurance money, but the insurance company refused to pay and cancelled his policy.

It was at this time that Maud Marsh was taken ill, with the familiar symptoms which had marked the cases of Mrs. Spink and Bessie Taylor. The unfortunate Maud became so ill that she was removed to hospital. Here the doctors were at a loss to know what was the matter with her, but, as she was away from her supposed husband's attention, she gradually recovered and was sent home.

Almost immediately there was a recurrence of the mysterious illness. Stoker was called in and once more professed himself completely baffled. The services of a nurse were engaged, while the patient's mother, who was very worried, also arrived to help.

Meanwhile Chapman insisted on preparing the patient's food and drink, and it was noticed that whenever she took any her condition became worse. When Mrs. Marsh and the nurse refreshed themselves with a brandy and soda which had been prepared for the sick woman, they were both immediately seized with painful attacks of vomiting and diarrhoea.

Mrs. Marsh then summoned her own doctor, a Dr. Grapel, of Croydon, and on examining the patient he came to the conclusion that she was being poisoned. He telegraphed Dr. Stoker to this effect, telling him to look out for arsenic. But it was too late. Chapman, having evidently taken fright at Dr. Grapel's visit, administered a stronger dose than usual, which brought about the sudden end of the patient. This happened on October 22, 1902. Because of Dr.

Grapel's message, Dr. Stoker refused to give a death certificate.

A post-mortem examination of the body took place, as a result of which more than twenty grains of antimony were discovered. At the coroner's inquest the chemist Davidson, who read of the case in the newspapers, remembered selling the tartar-emetic to Chapman in 1897 and came forward to assist the authorities. A week or so later Chapman was arrested and charged with the murder of Maud Marsh.

He decided to plead not guilty. Among the articles found by the police in his possession were various medical books treating on poisons and, strangely enough, a book written by Berry, the executioner, giving details of his career as a hangman.

The trial opened before Mr. Justice Grantham at the Old Bailey on March 16, 1903, and lasted for four days.

One extraordinary effect of antimony—and it was a novel discovery then—is that, if it is administered in the lifetime of the person, it preserves the body in a remarkable degree, so that even several years after death the body of the deceased person is easily recognisable. This was confirmed by Dr. Stevenson, the Home Office pathologist, under whose supervision the remains of Mrs. Spink and Bessie Taylor were exhumed. From the witness-box he described what he saw when the lid of Mrs. Spink's coffin was removed by the grave in the cemetery at Leytonstone. "The body was altogether remarkable," deposed Dr. Stevenson. "The face and head were those of a woman who might have been coffined that day, from the appearance. Even the eyes were unruptured, a very unusual circumstance. There was not the least difficulty in recognising her."

The judge summed up strongly against the prisoner, and after an absence of only eleven minutes the jury returned a verdict of guilty. He received the death sentence, with which the Home Secretary refused to interfere, and he was duly hanged.

There is no doubt that he was a sadistic maniac, who met his just deserts. It was later discovered that, before he came to England, he had married a woman in Poland and had beheaded her. Yet he died protesting his innocence to the last. When asked if he wished to see any of his friends, he replied bitterly, "I have none."

The trial of Severin Klosowski, alias George Chapman, is of unique interest for three reasons. First, because of the discovery which enabled the Home Office pathologist to show the peculiar power of antimony and how it preserves the human body after death. Secondly, it was the first trial in which it was found possible, as well as legal, to bring forward evidence of two other persons who had died by the poison administered to them by the accused. Thirdly, the trial led the police authorities to believe that the Borough poisoner was the same person as one of the most notorious figures in the annals of modern crime. That is to say, they sought to identify him with the mysterious murderer of Whitechapel who is popularly known as 'Jack the Ripper'.

While it is true that the mystery of the 'Ripper' murders has never been officially solved, the grounds for supposing that this sadistic Pole was the author of them are very strong. These murders took place in Whitechapel during the years 1888 and 1889. The victim was invariably a prostitute, who was killed at night with a sharp knife, her throat being cut and the lower part of her body horribly mutilated. Chapman was living in Whitechapel or within easy reach.

It was thought that the Ripper had medical knowledge; Chapman had certainly been a student of medicine. According to his wife, Lucy Baderski, Chapman was often out until three or four o'clock in the morning at the time the murders were committed. The description of Jack the Ripper as to height, complexion and curled moustache might be exactly applied to Chapman.

Again, there were American expressions in the callous messages which the Ripper sent the police: Chapman liked to pass himself off as an American and was in the habit of indulging in grim pleasantries of language.

Finally, the murders ceased in 1890, but between that year and 1892 similar murders occurred in the locality of Jersey City during the period that Chapman was living there. The Jersey

City murders ceased at the time Chapman left to return to England.

Chief Inspector Abberline of Scotland Yard, who had charge of the investigation into the Whitechapel murders, was quite convinced that Chapman and Jack the Ripper were identical. His theory was that when Chapman returned from America he came to the conclusion that the 'Ripper' type of murder was too dangerous, and he consequently turned to poisoning as a safer mode of killing.

3. THE BRIDES-IN-THE-BATH CASE

WITHOUT doubt one of the most extraordinary modern criminals was George Joseph Smith, the central figure in the notorious 'Brides-in-the-Bath' case, which shook Britain during the First World War. Smith was a lady-killer in the literal as well as the general sense. Possessed of a remarkable and, as some thought, an uncanny power to fascinate women, he simply treated them as a commercial proposition. If it was necessary to marry them and then kill them in the achievement of his object, he did not hesitate to do so. He had disposed of three of his wives in this manner by drowning them, or causing them to drown, in their baths, before he was brought to justice.

It was with the murder of the first of these brides, Bessie Mundy, that he was charged at the Old Bailey. At this time he was forty-three, and the details of his life as revealed at the trial consisted almost entirely of the exploitation of women in one way or another.

Smith was born in Bethnal Green in 1872, the son of respectable parents. From an early age he seems to have displayed criminal tendencies. He was sent to a reformatory when he was nine and remained there for seven years. Before he was twenty he had served two terms of imprisonment for theft. His mother despaired of him, prophesying—correctly, as it turned out—that he would die in his boots! Yet he was not without talent and he showed interest in better things than petty crime. He was genuinely fond of poetry, especially

Shakespeare, and he could play the piano and draw quite well. For a time he worked as a gymnastic instructor, but he soon discovered his real bent, which was with women. He began by attracting good-looking servant girls, whom he placed in situations by supplying them with fictitious references, then persuaded them to steal for him. Detected in this vile practice, he got twelve months hard labour.

On coming out of prison he went to Leicester, where he opened a bakery business. Here he met a girl named Beatrice Thornhill, whom he married in the name of 'George Love'. When the bakery venture failed, as it did a few months later, George brought his wife to London and forced her to take various situations, posing as her late employer, and then to steal for him. Unfortunately for her, she was caught and paid the price with a conviction for larceny. When she was released, however, she got her own back on her husband, whom she encountered by chance looking into a shop window. She handed him over to the police, and this time he got two years.

During the next decade his career followed this well-defined pattern. He would 'marry' the victim under an assumed name and, when he had got hold of all her money, would shamelessly abandon her. It did not matter that his haul consisted of the woman's entire life savings.

It was in 1910 that, in the guise of 'Mr. Henry Williams', a picture restorer, he met and 'married' Miss Mundy, the daughter of a deceased bank manager in Clifton. She had a small income of about £100 a year from capital which he could not touch, since it was held in trust for her. But he did contrive to lay hands on accumulated arrears of income to the amount of £138. He then absconded, leaving behind a cruel letter in which he accused poor Bessie Mundy of having given him 'a certain disease'.

Bessie heard nothing more of her errant husband until eighteen months later, when she happened to see him on the esplanade in Weston-super-Mare. Instead of handing him over to the police, like Beatrice Thornhill, she consented to go off and spend the night with him. Soon they were living together again in a rented house at Herne Bay. Soon afterwards he persuaded her to execute a will in his favour leaving him assets to the value of £2,500, which represented her capital. Five days later a doctor, summoned to the house, found Bessie lying naked in the bath with her head under water. She was dead.

At the inquest the cause of death was found by the coroner's jury to have been accidental. Having buried her in a pauper's grave, Smith obtained probate of his late wife's will and succeeded in converting her securities into cash.

Twice during the next two and a half years this apparent accident was repeated. In the autumn of 1913 Smith met a buxom young nurse named Alice Burnham outside a Nonconformist chapel at Southsea, where he went, as the prosecuting counsel said at his trial, not to pray but to 'prey' on young women of simple faith. A few weeks later they were married, this being the only one of his numerous ladies whom Smith married under his real name. He then succeeded in extracting a sum of £104 from the girl's father, which he had been keeping for her. He also insured her life for £500. In the following month they went to Blackpool and took lodgings from a landlady named Mrs. Crossley, Smith making sure beforehand that they had a bath.

On the night of December 12, 1913, the landlady saw water coming through the ceiling of her room. At this time Mrs. Smith was taking a bath in the bathroom above. Soon after this the husband, who claimed to have been out buying some eggs for their supper, returned. The verdict of the coroner's jury was the same as in the previous 'accident'.

Like her immediate predecessor the dead woman was buried in a pauper's grave, while her husband, after weeping copious crocodile tears at the inquest, went off to collect the insurance money, which in the circumstances was paid over without question.

Almost exactly a year later Mr. Burnham, the late Mrs. Smith's father in Southsea, and Mr. Crossley, the landlady's husband in Blackpool, were each struck by a headline they saw in a Sunday newspaper, 'Bride's Tragic Fate On Day After Wedding'. The bride in question, Miss Margaret Lofty, had been found dead in her bath in a lodging-house in Highgate by her distracted husband, whose name was given as John Lloyd. "That is Smith," said Mr. Burnham and Mr. Crossley to themselves. And so it was. They sent the newspaper cuttings to the police. As for the unfortunate Margaret Lofty, she was the best born of all Smith's brides—her father was a clergyman—but she was also the poorest and brought her husband only £19. Smith was arrested as he was about to enter a solicitor's office with a view to proving her will.

His trial opened before Mr. Justice Scrutton at the Central Criminal Court on June 22, 1915, and lasted nine days. Sir Archibald Bodkin led for the Crown and Sir Edward Marshall Hall for the defence. It was the largest and most important trial since that of Palmer, the poisoner, sixty years before, and in respect of the amount of evidence which was put in it was unique.

The prisoner's defence, eloquently put forward by his counsel—Smith refused to go into the witness-box—was that none of the bodies bore any marks of violence, and it would be impossible for Smith to have committed the crime without leaving marks of violence and signs of a struggle.

But the jury did not accept this view and they brought in a verdict of guilty. Smith was duly sentenced to death and executed.

There was no doubt in Marshall Hall's mind that his client was responsible for the deaths of the three brides—but not by drowning them in the manner suggested by the prosecution at the trial. On the contrary, the advocate was convinced that Smith had hypnotised them and that they had lost their lives while under the influence of hypnosis.

4. THE FRENCH BLUEBEARD

NO murder trial within living memory has probably aroused more widespread international interest than that of Henri Landru at Versailles in 1921. In their magnitude and horror the crimes of which this man was eventually convicted have been matched only by the legendary exploits of the original

Bluebeard in medieval France, who killed his wives and hid them in a locked room.

At the Versailles trial the prosecution established that Landru had written to no fewer than 283 women proposing marriage, and had murdered ten of these unfortunate women and the child of one of them. The bodies of the victims were subsequently burned by Landru in a stove, and it was the discovery of their calcined remains which constituted the strongest link in the chain of circumstantial evidence against him. No wonder that public indignation at the time became so worked up against this arch-criminal, and that the most elaborate security precautions were taken to prevent his being lynched by the infuriated spectators in court.

At the time of his arrest in 1919 the accused man was fifty years of age. He came of respectable working-class parents, and had been brought up in a decent God-fearing home. He was a chorister and censer boy in his parish church, but at a fairly early age, in the words of the trial judge, he adopted "more profane pursuits". He seduced the daughter of his cousin, who had a child by him, but later married her and they had three more children. After doing his military service, he took various jobs as a clerk, book-keeper and the like, but soon decided to become a professional swindler.

He specialised in the most susceptible type of women, widows between thirty-eight and fifty, who had their own furniture and a few thousand francs in the bank. As a rule he got into touch with them through matrimonial agencies or matrimonial advertisements in the newspapers usually under an assumed name. He was a practised lover, and, having become engaged to his prospective victim, would persuade her to part with her furniture and valuables on the ground that she would not need these after their marriage. Her money he promised to invest at a higher rate of interest than she was getting from the bank. He would then sell the furniture and disappear. In the majority of cases he was successful. In the exceptional case when he was caught he went to prison. When he could not get rid of his victim in any other way he killed her and disposed of the remains at one of his country villas near Paris.

Landru was most business-like in his operations. In his notebooks he entered details of the 283 replies he received to his advertisements. But he was also incredibly mean and greedy. He would hoard the papers, identity cards and even the linen and dresses of his victims.

The police succeeded in tracing all but eleven persons on Landru's list. They had little to tell beyond stories of how they had been robbed of their possessions under promise of marriage. The missing victims were as follows:

1–2—Mme. Cuchet, a widow, aged thirty-nine, and her son André, aged eighteen. She worked in a lingerie store in Paris. Early in 1914 she met Landru, who then had a garage and motor repair business. Young André Cuchet brought his bicycle to be mended and then asked Landru for a job as a mechanic. Landru said he would have to get permission from the boy's parents as he was a minor. In this way he met the mother, proposed marriage, and induced her to come and live with him. After January, 1915, nothing further was heard of either mother or son. Meanwhile Landru had obtained possession of her jewels, furniture and securities.

3—Mme. Laborde-Lisse, widow, aged forty-seven, who came from Buenos Aires. She met Landru in June, 1915, and left her Paris apartment a few weeks later, telling the porter that she was going to get married. She withdrew money from the bank and realised her securities, which she handed over to Landru. She disappeared a month later.

4—Mme. Guillon, a widow, aged fifty-one, formerly a governess. She had inherited 22,000 francs and met Landru, who called himself George Petit, in May, 1915, through a matrimonial advertisement. She disappeared soon afterwards. Landru sold her furniture and withdrew her money from the bank by means of a forged signature.

5—Mme. Heon, widow, aged fifty-five. She met Landru through a matrimonial advertisement in September, 1915. He sold her furniture in the same month, and then took her to live at the Villa Ermitage at Gambais, near Versailles. No more was heard of her until the trial.

6—Mme. Colomb, widow, aged forty-four. She was a well-dressed and good-looking woman, who worked as a typist in a Paris office. She had a nest-egg of 10,000 francs. She also had a lover who was beginning to tire of her. Hence she replied enthusiastically to an advertisement she saw which told her that a widower, aged forty-three, "with comfortable income, affectionate, serious and moving in good society", desired to meet a widow with a view to marriage. In December, 1916, she went to live with Landru and told her mother and sister she was getting married and moving to Nice. In fact she went to the Villa Ermitage, from which she never returned.

7—Mlle. Babelay, domestic servant, aged nineteen. Unlike the other victims, she had no money. Landru saw her crying on the platform of the Paris Underground in January, 1917. He took her home to his Paris apartment and later to Gambais, where he described her as his niece. She disappeared in April, 1917.

8—Mme. Buisson, widow, aged forty-four. She visited Gambais in August, 1917, and disappeared soon afterwards.

9—Mme. Jaume, aged thirty-eight, separated from her husband. She started divorce proceedings in order to marry Landru, and went to Gambais in November, 1917. She was last seen in the same month.

10—Mme. Pascal, divorcée, aged thirty-three. She was a dressmaker of easy morals, who fell in love with Landru. She disappeared in 1917.

11—Mme. Marchadier, a single woman of illegitimate birth who kept a Paris lodging-house and styled herself 'Madame'. She gave up her house, sold most of her furniture and went to Gambais in January, 1919, disappearing the same month.

The families of several of these victims had written to the Mayor of Gambais, asking for his help. It was the sister of Mme. Buisson, Mlle. Lacoste, who happened to see Landru buying a china dinner service in a Paris store in company with another woman, and recognised him as the man with whom her sister had gone away. She informed the police and Landru was arrested a few days later. A thorough search of the Gambais villa revealed the remains of three skeletons, five feet

M

and six hands. Portions of human flesh were also found in a near-by lake.

After a long preliminary hearing before the examining magistrate, Landru was brought up for trial before the Assize Court in Versailles on November 7, 1921. He was defended by Maître Moro-Gaffieri.

Although he repeatedly protested during the trial that his relations with these women were of a strictly business nature concerned with the sale of their furniture, there is little doubt that he made each of them his mistress before killing her. The explanation of their disappearance given by his counsel was that Landru was really engaged in the white slave traffic, and that the women had in consequence gone to South America. But no one on the jury believed this story, which has no evidence to substantiate it.

Landru was examined by three doctors, who gave it as their expert opinion that he was not suffering from any form of paranoia. The prisoner thanked them in open court for their trouble. The "monstrosity of the crimes of which I am accused," he declared, "extraordinary even for the most perverse man, can be explained only by the most marked insanity. In acknowledging that I am sane they are thus proclaiming my innocence."

The jury did not accept the prisoner's interpretation of this expert medical opinion. They found him guilty of premeditated murder. Although their verdict rested solely on circumstantial evidence, there can be little if any doubt of its justice. Like the notorious G. J. Smith, the 'brides-in-the-bath' murderer, Landru lived by robbing unsuspecting women of their possessions. Like the English criminal, too, Landru killed his victims when there was no other method of keeping them quiet.

It is not known how much he got from his victims who lived. Those who died yielded only 35,000 francs (£1,750) between them. Landru was publicly guillotined in Versailles at dawn on February 2, 1922. "I want neither pity nor mercy," he said at the end. History will accord him none.

5. THE 'LONELY HEARTS' MURDERS

ONE morning in November, 1948, the postman delivered a letter at a home for crippled children in a small town in the United States. Bearing the postmark of a New York suburb, the Bronx, it was addressed to twenty-seven-year-old Mrs. Martha Beck who was in charge of the home at Pensacola, Florida. Sent as a practical joke by an old school-mate whom she had recently met at a party, the letter was from a 'Lonely Hearts Club', which Mrs. Beck was invited to join. Her response to the invitation put in motion a chain of happenings which was eventually to lead Mrs. Beck, with her confederate in crime, to the electric chair in New York's Sing Sing Prison.

The envelope contained a pamphlet headed, "Are you lonely or shy? Then join Mother Dinene's Friendly Club for Lonely Hearts." Mrs. Beck read on. "Mother Dinene has helped hundreds of women to find suitable mates, carefully selected from the long list of lonely but eligible men who are seeking —even as you are seeking—to find true happiness in a blissful marriage. Many of the men on her list are gay, witty, charming, and have good positions or are independently wealthy. Why should you not meet such men? Mother Dinene will show you the way."

The pamphlet contained several blurred photographs of allegedly satisfied customers of 'Mother Dinene'. On the last page there were instructions how to join the Club. All any interested woman had to do was to send a description of herself, accompanied by five dollars in cash, and the obliging 'Mother Dinene' would do the rest.

In her reply Mrs. Beck stated that she was "witty, vivacious and oozed personality". She elaborated that she was a trained nurse with a good post and had her own "pleasant apartment". She might have added, though she did not, that she was divorced with two children, that she was a heavy, physically overdeveloped woman, that she had been the victim of a hideous criminal assault as a girl, and that she had once worked in a mortuary.

Some weeks later Martha received another letter, this time from a man on 'Mother Dinene's' books who lived in Brooklyn. It was full of airy compliments, and the writer suggested a meeting soon. His name was Raymond Fernandez, and he was thirty-five years of age. He had been born of Spanish parents in Hawaii, and was therefore an American citizen. He had some claims to good looks of the Charles Boyer type, but they were marred by a three-inch scar on his forehead, the result of a head injury which he had received while working as a seaman in the West Indies and which had unquestionably affected his brain.

He was, in fact, a criminal adventurer who had already served a term in gaol for theft and also had at least one undetected murder to his credit. At his trial he admitted to having seduced over a hundred women to whom he had been introduced through 'Lonely Hearts' clubs, frequently defrauding them of money or possessions in the process. He had contracted syphilis, had wild dreams, was convinced he had hypnotic power over women, and was a student of voodoo and forms of 'black magic'. As soon as he appeared at Pensacola he had no difficulty in adding Martha Beck to his list of conquests.

Fernandez had recently returned from a trip to Spain, where incidentally he had a wife and four children. He had gone there with another 'Lonely Hearts' victim, a Mrs. Jane Thompson, with whom he travelled as his wife and to whom he administered a fatal dose of digitalis.

On his return to New York he had gone to the apartment where Mrs. Thompson lived with her ailing mother, Mrs. Wilson, to whom he produced a forged will and other documents making him the sole heir of Mrs. Thompson's property. He then moved into the apartment and was good enough to allow Mrs. Wilson to continue to stay there. But not for long. Martha's behaviour with Fernandez in Pensacola came to the notice of her employers, and on her return from a fortnight's leave in New York, which she had spent with her lover, she found that her services were no longer required. She then went back to New York and settled down with Fernandez, having first got rid of Mrs. Wilson by persuading her to go and live with her son.

Martha, who was infatuated with Fernandez and willing to do anything he asked, now entered wholeheartedly into his 'Lonely Hearts' activities. During the next twelve months they netted considerable sums of money from several victims. Two of them Fernandez bigamously 'married' with the connivance of Martha, who posed as his sister. The second of these, whose name was Mrs. Myrtle Young from Arkansas, was poisoned with an overdose of barbiturates. She yielded 4,000 dollars and a motor-car. At the time no foul play was suspected.

The next victim was an elderly widow, Mrs. Janet Fay, who came to spend the night in the New York apartment and was clubbed to death with a hammer by Martha. At her trial she claimed she caught Mrs. Fay 'making up' to Fernandez. "Everything went black, and the next thing I knew, she was dead." The body was placed in a trunk and later taken to a house which the killers rented in another part of New York. The remains were then buried in the cellar. Meanwhile Martha succeeded in cashing cheques endorsed by the murdered woman to the value of 3,000 dollars.

At this stage the killers made a fatal mistake. They had a sheet of paper which bore Mrs. Fay's signature, and on this they typed a letter to her stepdaughter, Mrs. Spencer, asking her to send her various personal belongings. Since Mrs. Fay did not own a typewriter and did not know how to type, Mrs. Spencer's suspicions were aroused and she took the letter to the police.

Meanwhile Martha and Raymond had got another unfortunate woman into their clutches. This was an attractive widow of forty-one, Mrs. Delphine Downing, who lived in Grand Rapids, Michigan, with her baby daughter named Rainelle. Raymond and Martha drove to Michigan and soon Raymond was on terms of intimacy with the widow. As usual, he also persuaded her to transfer her assets to him under promise of marriage. Then she thought she was pregnant. Martha kindly offered to help and gave her what appeared to be a drug to procure an abortion. Actually it was a strong sleeping-draught.

Raymond then killed her with a revolver while she slept.

When the child Rainelle kept crying for her mother, Martha filled a washtub with water and held the child down until she drowned. Afterwards they buried mother and child in the cellar, as they had done with Mrs. Fay in New York. But by this time the neighbours had become suspicious, and before they could leave Michigan, Martha and Raymond were arrested.

Since there is no capital punishment in the State of Michigan, the authorities there did not object to surrendering the prisoners to the New York police, who demanded their extradition on the charge of murdering Mrs. Fay, applying the accepted English test of the McNaughten Rules.

On June 9, 1949, their trial opened before Judge Pecora, of the New York State Supreme Court, sitting in Bronx County. Both prisoners ran the defence of insanity, but Fernandez later altered his plea to guilty to being an accessory after the fact.

The trial, which lasted for forty-four days, was concerned largely with the evidence of psychiatrists. The defence stressed the other murders and referred to abnormalities and perversions practised by the prisoners. But it was the evidence of the State psychiatrist which was accepted. He found both prisoners sane.

As for Martha, he declared "she knew she was directing the hammer to Mrs. Fay's skull and she knew, when she had done that, she was causing damage to Mrs. Fay's skull. In my opinion, it was impossible for this woman to have amnesia and not recall before or after that she had a weapon".

The jury, after retiring for a whole night, found both defendants guilty of first-degree murder. They both lodged appeals, which were discussed by the New York Court of Appeals eleven months later. On March 8, 1951, they were electrocuted in Sing Sing.

The case caused a sensation throughout America. Besides focusing attention on the scandal of the Lonely Hearts Club, it brought up the whole question of crime and abnormality.

Martha subsequently asserted that it was not her hand which struck the fatal blow that killed Janet Fay, and some grounds for this belief are provided by the fact that she was left-handed, while Mrs. Fay was killed with a right-handed blow. Even so, this could not, in my opinion, have relieved her of criminal responsibility for the murder.

I am convinced that, under the present law, Martha Beck and Raymond Fernandez were rightly convicted. Whether the law should be revised, however, is another matter.

6. THE ACID BATH KILLER

THERE can be no trial within living memory—saving those of Landru, the French Bluebeard, and of Christie—which for sheer horror surpasses that of John George Haigh. He was charged at Lewes Assizes in 1949 with the murder of Mrs. Durand-Deacon, an elderly widow, who lived in the same private hotel at Kensington. The accused man admitted to having killed this woman and seven other people besides, draining off some of their blood and drinking it in each case, and the disposing of the bodies in sulphuric acid. Two of the alleged victims may well have been the products of Haigh's disordered imagination, but it is certain that he killed the others. He pleaded insanity as the term is understood in English law.

Haigh, who was shortly to celebrate his fortieth birthday in the condemned cell in Wandsworth Prison, occupied an adjoining table to Mrs. Durand-Deacon in the hotel where they both lived. He noticed that she had some valuable jewellery, and he was very hard up at the time. A man of apparent charm, he succeeded in ingratiating himself with this widow. One day she disappeared from the hotel.

She had a friend, a Mrs. Lane, who also lived there, and Mrs. Lane, who had recently seen them talking together, told Haigh she was going to report her friend's absence to the police. Haigh offered to drive Mrs. Lane to the police and in fact he took her to Chelsea Police Station for this purpose.

Police suspicions were soon directed towards Haigh when a routine check revealed that he had several previous convictions for crimes involving dishonesty. The suspicions were confirmed when the police searched a storehouse in Leopold Road, Crawley, belonging to a firm of which Haigh claimed to be a director. Among other things they found a revolver and a receipt from a firm of cleaners for a Persian lamb coat. The coat was traced and identified as belonging to Mrs. Durand-Deacon.

At first Haigh denied that he had any notion of Mrs. Durand-Deacon's whereabouts. He repeated his denial at a second interview with the police, but at the third meeting he changed his tactics and came out with an astonishing confession.

"I will tell you all about it," he said. "Mrs. Durand-Deacon no longer exists. She has disappeared completely and no trace of her can ever be found again. You will find the sludge which remains at Leopold Road." Then, by way of an afterthought, he added, "How can you prove murder if there is no body?."

Haigh does not seem to have appreciated that production of the victim's body is unnecessary to establish a charge of murder. Indeed, only a year previously a ship's steward, named James Camb, had been convicted for killing at sea a passenger whose body was never found.

Haigh was also in error when he claimed that all tell-tale traces of his latest crime had disappeared. No less than 475 lbs. of grease and earth were sent from Crawley to Scotland Yard for laboratory inspection. They revealed quantities of body fat, gall-stones and bones, all clearly of human origin. They also included a set of dentures which was recovered intact. This was later indentified as Mrs. Durand-Deacon's.

Like Landru in France, Haigh came of a respectable family and was brought up in a homely, religious atmosphere. As a boy he sang in his church choir, also like the French Bluebeard, and for a time he used to play the organ in Wakefield Cathedral. Soon after leaving school he discovered, as he himself put it, that there were easier ways of making a living than working long hours in an office. He began by defrauding several hire-purchase companies of sums of money in respect of motor-car sales. He was caught and got fifteen months.

Later he obtained more than £3,000 by shares in bogus

companies, posing as a solicitor with estates to wind up. This
time he got four years penal servitude. Released on licence in
1940, he became a fire-watcher in Civil Defence, but was soon
in trouble again for stealing from property it was his duty to
protect. He completed his third sentence in 1943.

Soon afterwards Haigh met a young man named William
McSwan, whom he had known before the war when McSwan
was managing an amusement arcade. McSwan, who owned
some house property in London, and still seems to have
retained an interest in the fun-fair business, confided in Haigh
his intention of going underground in order to avoid National
Service. This seems to have given Haigh the idea of killing
him.

At that time Haigh had a basement workshop in Gloucester
Road, and one day in September, 1944, McSwan brought a
pin-table there for repair. According to Haigh, he hit him on
the head and later put his body in a disused water tub, into
which he poured sulphuric acid. Before doing this he claimed
to have drained some of McSwan's blood into a mug and
drunk it.

Although the jury at his trial refused to believe that he was
legally insane, there is no doubt that Haigh was mentally
abnormal. Blood and bleeding seem to have been an obsession
with him, although there is no evidence to show that this
morbid preoccupation was connected with any form of sexual
perversion.

Nor indeed is there any evidence that Haigh actually drank
his victims' blood. We only have Haigh's word for it. In the
sole case, that of Mrs. Durand-Deacon, in which the defence
might have produced the vessel which Haigh claimed to have
used for this purpose, they did not do so. But there is certainly
the possibility.

While awaiting trial he told a psychiatrist that his mother
used to correct him during childhood by smacking his hand
with the bristles of a hairbrush. On one occasion, he said, this
punishment drew blood, which he sucked and enjoyed to such
an extent that he later deliberately cut his finger to gratify the
taste he had acquired. He also admitted to dreams of fantasy

which preceded the murders, pretending to see a forest of crucifixes turning into trees and oozing blood, which he was urged to drink by a man who caught the blood from each tree in a cup.

Several months after the killing of McSwan he murdered McSwan's parents, and through forged deeds was able to obtain control of their assets, as he had done in the case of the son. Haigh had told McSwan's parents that their son had gone away because his call-up was imminent. This family yielded him £4,000.

The McSwans must have had few friends, for their disappearance was never reported to the police. It was Haigh himself who revealed the secret when he was arrested.

His next victims were a Dr. Archibald Henderson and his wife, whom he met in 1947 in answer to a newspaper advertisement of a house they wished to sell. Early in 1948 he shot them both in the store-room at Crawley with a revolver, subsequently dissolving their bodies in sulphuric acid. From them he secured more than £2,000.

The unfortunate Mrs. Durand-Deacon followed a year later. Haigh persuaded her to accompany him to Crawley on the pretext of witnessing the experimental manufacture of plastic finger-nails, a project in which she had expressed interest.

Haigh also claimed to have killed an elderly woman and a youth during the last two years of the war, but the police were unable to test the truth of this statement.

Haigh was tried at Lewes Assizes by Mr. Justice Humphreys. The Attorney-General, then Sir Hartley Shawcross, led for the prosecution and had no difficulty in convincing the jury that Haigh had killed Mrs. Durand-Deacon.

Haigh's confession to this and the other murders was read out in court and used by his counsel, Sir David Maxwell Fyfe, to support the plea that he was insane at the time. The proceedings thus involved the application of the so-called McNaughten Rules.

Laid down at the time of the trial of Daniel McNaughten for the murder of Sir Robert Peel's private secretary, Mr. Drummond, more than a century ago, these Rules briefly are to the effect that an insanity plea can succeed only where the defence can show that the accused did not know what he was doing, or that if he did know he was not conscious that what he was doing was wrong.

Haigh did not go into the witness-box to give evidence on his own behalf. His only witness was a Harley Street psychiatrist, Dr. Henry Yellowlees, who had examined Haigh in prison and stated that in his opinion he was a paranoiac.

However, when pressed by the Attorney-General this witness was obliged to admit that in his opinion, too, the prisoner must have known that what he did was punishable by the law of the country, and therefore wrong. With this admission the case for the defence collapsed. The jury found Haigh guilty and he was duly hanged.

Haigh murdered for money, and his murders were facilitated by his abnormal state of mind. His conduct was certainly not that of an entirely sane or rational man. Yet he could not be considered insane on the construction of the McNaughten Rules in his case.

Whether these Rules are satisfactory is another matter. There is a growing body of opinion in this country which would like to see them changed, perhaps to cover such cases as Haigh's and those of similar multiple murderers.

V. THE CASE FOR AND AGAINST FLOGGING

V. THE CASE FOR AND AGAINST FLOGGING

AS a sentence of the court in Britain, flogging came to an end in 1948 under the provisions of the Criminal Justice Act. Its abolition was the result of the recommendations of a Departmental Committee appointed before the war by the Home Secretary, then Sir John Simon, to consider the whole question of corporal punishment in our penal system and presided over by the Hon. (later Sir) Edward Cadogan. Today in this country whipping can be legally awarded only for certain types of prison offence, such as a violent assault upon a warder, and then only by order of the prison authorities. It was announced recently that a Dartmoor convict had received twelve strokes of the 'cat' for assaulting two warders.

When the courts formerly ordered an offender to be flogged, what did this punishment involve? Many people, including some who demand the reintroduction of flogging for crimes of violence, have mistaken notions on the subject. It is therefore necessary to understand the precise implications of this punishment.

The instrument used in flogging was either the birch, sometimes inaccurately called the 'birch rod', or else a particular kind of whip known as the 'cat-o'-nine-tails'. When passing sentences of corporal punishment the court invariably directed which of these two forms it should take.

Punishment by the 'cat' was limited to males of eighteen years and over. The maximum number of strokes permitted was fifty under sentence of the court and thirty-six (now reduced to eighteen) for offences against prison discipline. They must all be administered at one time and within six months of the date of sentence. In the event of the interruption of the flogging on medical grounds the remainder of the punishment must be remitted.

Although flogging in this country is no longer inflicted with the barbarity that it once was, it must nevertheless be regarded as a severe punishment. Before a prisoner can be flogged he must be medically examined with great care and notified physically fit. He must not suffer from any physical disease or weakness. However, this does not exempt him on account of physical disability, provided no serious or permanent injury is likely to result. In 1928 a man suffering from infantile paralysis was flogged.

The 'birch rod' used for judicial whippings is not a rod or cane, but a bundle of birch twigs, not unlike the type of broom used by a gardener for sweeping up leaves. The twigs are bound together at the thick end to form a handle, and the remainder is left free so that the loose ends of the twigs spray out. The specifications of the birch used for adults are as follows: overall length, 48 inches; length of handle, 22 inches; circumference of spray at centre, 7 inches; total weight, 12 ounces. For use in administering corporal punishment to boys under sixteen birches of rather smaller dimensions have been specified.

Contrary to a widely held but erroneous belief, the birch was never soaked in brine to make the punishment more painful. It was, however, sometimes soaked in water before use. But the object was merely to make it supple. The twigs of a birch which has been kept for some time are apt to become brittle and break off during use, unless they are first moistened.

The 'cat', on the other hand, is a whip of nine lashes. These lashes consists of fine whipcord closely bound at the ends to prevent fraying, and attached to a short cloth-covered handle. Its precise specifications are as follows: length of lashes, 33 inches; length of handle, 19¾ inches; weight of handle, 6¾ ounces; weight of lashes, 2¼ ounces; total weight, 9 ounces. Lashes made of leather are not employed, nor are they now knotted or weighted in any way. Nevertheless, as these details reveal, the 'cat' is a formidable instrument and is certainly no light punishment when laid on by a prison officer who knows his duty.

A prisoner ordered for flogging is strapped to an apparatus

Picture Post

Above: THE BOY'S PONY
    AS USED IN
    CLERKENWELL
    PRISON, 1874

Right: LANDRU

Picture Post

Juvenile Court

known as a triangle, which has been described as a heavier and more solid form of easel used to carry a blackboard in a school-room. His feet are strapped to the base of the front legs of the triangle. If he is to receive the 'cat', his hands are raised above his head and strapped to the upper part of the apparatus. A leather belt is also placed round his loins and a leather collar round his neck, so as to protect his kidneys and spinal cord from the possible injurious effects of any misdirected stroke. If he is to be birched, he is bent over a pad placed between the front legs of the triangle and his hands are secured by straps attached to its back legs. In both cases he is screened, by canvas sheeting, so that he cannot see the officer who is administering the punishment.

For this duty the Cadogan Committee were satisfied that prison governors always take care to select a steady and experienced man who can be relied upon to administer the punishment 'dispassionately'. He receives a special allowance of 2s. 6d. for his work (5s. in Scotland).

In English prisons the method of administration is as follows: the birch is applied across the buttocks, on the bare flesh. The 'cat' is applied across the back, also on the bare flesh, so that the ends of the lashes fall in the region of the right shoulder-blade.

In Scotland the procedure was slightly different. Flogging, whether by birch or 'cat', is administered by two officers, one standing on each side of the prisoner and each delivering alternate strokes. Nor is the prisoner screened to prevent his seeing the officers administering the punishment.

In all cases the Prison Governor and Medical Officer must be present. The strokes are delivered at deliberate intervals, the time being counted by the Chief Officer of the Prison. The normal rate is not faster than fifteen strokes a minute, which means that the culprit has time to appreciate the full effect of one stroke on his person before he receives the next. The Medical Officer stands in a position where he can see the prisoner's face, and he has complete discretion to stop the punishment at any time if he considers that on medical grounds it is undesirable for it to be continued.

It is commonly supposed that the birch causes much less pain than the 'cat'. That is incorrect. Those who are in a position to know assure me that as it was administered in prisons a birching is almost, if not quite, as painful as a flogging with the 'cat'. The wielder of either instrument delivers each stroke with the full force at his command and not infrequently draws blood.

On the other hand, it is quite untrue, as has sometimes been suggested, that prisoners often lose consciousness under the lash. Out of 343 cases of corporal punishment administered in English prisons during the period 1925–35, there were only nine in which the flogging was stopped on medical grounds before the full sentence could be carried out, and there were only four in which the prisoner had to be removed to hospital as a result of the punishment he had undergone.

The judicial flogging of boys is a much less terrifying business than that of adults. The punishment was almost always carried out immediately after the rising of the court, usually by a police constable, who bent the lad over a low bench or table. The boy's trousers were taken down and he received his punishment on the bare buttocks. A lighter birch was used than in the case of adults.

In Scotland an alternative for boys under fourteen was authorised in the shape of the tawse, a pliant leather strap divided at one end into several tongues. There the regulations prescribed that this punishment should be 'sufficiently severe to cause a repetition of it to be dreaded'. Maximum number of cuts permissible with birch or tawse was twelve up to the age of fourteen, and thirty-six cuts for boys between fourteen and sixteen. It is only fair to state that no credible evidence has been found to show that corporal punishment, painful as no doubt it is to the recipient, has produced any lasting physical consequences. The prisoner's flesh may exhibit a pattern of red weals for a time, but these traces of punishment soon disappear. Contrary to widespread opinion, the lashes of the 'cat' do not mark a man for life.

WHIPPING has been a mode of punishment in Britain since earliest times. Indeed, no other country, with the possible exception of Tsarist Russia, can point to such constant resort to the lash in its penal code. Until the beginning of the last century whipping was the customary penalty for all Common Law misdemeanours as well as for those statutory misdemeanours for which no punishment was specifically provided by statute. Men and women alike were whipped for such offences as vagrancy, theft, drunkenness, insanity, having illegitimate children, and sometimes even for smallpox.

The punishment was usually administered in public, either at the cart's tail or, later, at a public whipping-post. Indeed it was not until after 1861 that all sentences of judicial flogging had to be carried out in private. Judge Jeffreys's remarks to the executioner in sentencing a woman prisoner at the Old Bailey Sessions in 1678 for some petty theft have often been quoted. "Hangman," said this sanguinary judge, "I charge you to pay particular attention to this lady. Scourge her soundly, man. Scourge her till her blood runs down. It is Christmas, a cold time for madam to strip in. See that you warm her shoulders thoroughly."

Flogging was also the accepted punishment for a wide range of disciplinary offences in the armed forces of the Crown. The cat-o'-nine-tails was first used to whip English soldiers and sailors—tradition ascribes its introduction to King William III —and its use was widespread throughout the Services for nearly 200 years after the passing of the first Mutiny Act in 1689. This Act originally gave courts martial the power of inflicting corporal punishment to any extent. Sir Charles Napier, one of Wellington's generals and the historian of the Peninsular War, stated that he often saw from 600 to 1,000 lashes inflicted in consequence of regimental courts martial. And in those days a man who had suffered a part of his punishment was often brought from hospital, when his wounds were barely healed, to receive the remainder, "the greatest torture possible", in Napier's words. Military offences punishable with the 'cat' included mutiny, insubordination, striking a superior officer, drunkenness on duty, stealing from comrades and the unauthorised sale of arms or equipment.

In 1811 Sir Francis Burdett, M.P., who along with Lord Brougham led the parliamentary agitation for the abolition of flogging in the Army, called the attention of the House of Commons to the recent flogging of a private in the Liverpool militia, who had been condemned to receive 200 lashes merely for complaining along with others of the inferior quality of the bread served out to the regiment and afterwards writing a song about it.

But the incident which probably stirred the public imagination more than any other, was the flogging of Private Somerville of the Scots Greys in 1832. Somerville was believed by some of the officers of this regiment to be the author of an anonymous letter supporting the Reform Bill which appeared in a local newspaper. The writing of such a letter was not, of course, a military offence, but the officers decided to make an example of him. He was deliberately provoked into committing a technical act of disobedience during drill, and for this he was sentenced to 200 lashes by a regimental court martial.

In fact, he received 100, and he lived to describe the punishment in a remarkable book which he wrote, *The Autobiography of a Working Man*. A prisoner flogged with the 'cat' today probably experiences similar feelings during the first few strokes.

"Farrier Simpson took the cat as ordered; at least I believe so; I did not see him, but I felt an astounding sensation between the shoulders under my neck which went to my toe-nails in one direction, my finger-nails in another, and stung me to the heart as if a knife had gone through my body.

"The sergeant-major called in a loud voice 'One,' and I felt as if it would be kind of Simpson not to strike me in the same place again. He came on a second time, a few inches lower, and then I thought the former stroke was sweet and agreeable when compared with that one.

"The sergeant-major counted 'Two'. The cat was swung twice round the farrier's head again, and he came on somewhere about the right shoulder-blade, and the loud voice of the reckoner said, 'Three'.

"The shoulder-blade was as sensitive as any other part of the body, and when he came again on the left shoulder, and the voice called 'Four', I felt my flesh quiver in every nerve, from the scalp of my head to my toe-nails.

"The time between each stroke seemed so long as to be agonising and, yet the next came too soon."

The case of Private Somerville, along with that of a marine at Portsmouth, who died about the same period after receiving 134 lashes, led to the appointment of a Royal Commission on Military Punishments in 1836. Largely through the Duke of Wellington's evidence, the Commission did not recommend the abolition of flogging in the Services, merely its restriction. Abolition did not come about until the 'seventies.

The Duke of Wellington remained an uncompromising opponent of abolition throughout his life. "I have no idea of any great effort being produced by anything but the fear of immediate corporal punishment," he told the Royal Commission. "I must say that in hundreds of instances the very threat of the lash has prevented serious crimes."

Asked whether he could have established discipline in the Army without corporal punishment, Wellington replied, "No; it is out of the question . . . Having had this subject in contemplation for six or seven years, I have turned it over in my mind in every possible way, and I declare that I have not an idea of what can be substituted for it."

The amelioration of the ordinary criminal law in respect of flogging was more rapid than in the Services. After 1820 women were no longer allowed to be flogged, and after 1824 vagrants could be whipped only for second or subsequent offences, and the power to order this punishment was removed altogether from courts of summary jurisdiction. In 1843 the Commissioners on the Criminal Law submitted a report to Parliament in which they made it clear that they were opposed to the retention of whipping as a penalty for adult offenders.

"We think that, so far from extending this species of punishment," they wrote, "it would be better to reject it. . . . It is a punishment which is uncertain in point of severity, which inflicts an ignominious and indelible disgrace on the offender, and tends, we believe, to render him callous and greatly to obstruct his return to any honest course of life."

The Commissioners' recommendations resulted in a great consolidation of the criminal code in 1861. The effect of this legislation was to abolish corporal punishment for almost every offence in this country. Thereafter, whipping could only be ordered for the statutory crime of discharging a firearm at the Sovereign, a second or subsequent conviction for vagrancy, and—the two last seem to have been retained through an oversight—slaughtering horses without a licence and issuing a writ against a foreign Ambassador which might result in his arrest or in the distraint of his goods.

But it was not long before Parliament decided that it had gone too far. Flogging was restored as a punishment for certain offences, and it was also introduced for some new ones.

3

THE great revision and consolidation of our penal code which took place in 1861 resulted in the abolition of flogging as a judicial punishment for virtually every criminal offence except persistent vagrancy and discharging a firearm at the Sovereign. But there was soon a public outcry for the reintroduction of the 'cat'. In the latter part of 1862 an unusually large number of violent robberies took place in London. In many cases the violence took the form of garrotting, that is, attempting to choke or strangle the victim. The outbreak culminated in an attack on an M.P. This led, early in 1863, to a private member, Mr. Charles Adderley, later Lord Norton, introducing a Bill designed to empower the courts to add flogging to the penalties already available for garrotting and robbery with violence.

By the time the Bill came before Parliament, the wave of

violence had ebbed. The Home Secretary, Sir George Grey, spoke against its second reading in the Commons, describing it as "panic legislation after the panic had subsided". Nevertheless, the Bill passed into law as the Garrotters Act. It was re-enacted by the Larceny Act 1916, and remained on the statute book until its repeal, along with other flogging enactments, in 1948. It has never applied to Scotland.

It is frequently stated that garrotting was stamped out by the use of the lash as provided by this Act. This has even been repeated in the latest edition of the *Encyclopædia Britannica*. The facts are that garrotting was merely a phase of criminal activity which came and went with equal suddenness. The phase had already passed before the Garrotters Act became law.

On the other hand, robbery with violence, which the Act's flogging provisions were also designed to quell, actually increased. In 1862, the year of the incidents which led to the passing of the Act, sixty-five persons were convicted at the Old Bailey of this type of offence. In 1865 and 1866 the numbers, respectively, were seventy-six and seventy-three.

It is also sometimes said that the violent robberies perpetrated in Liverpool in the 'eighties and early 'nineties were stopped by the flogging sentences imposed by Mr. Justice Day. This judge was a great believer in the lash, and he frequently ordered it at Assizes. Yet at the end of the decade in which Mr. Justice Day tried to stamp out brutal crimes by flogging the number of robberies with violence was actually greater than it had been at the beginning. In the first three years of the period the total number of offenders was 176. In the last three years, after a prolonged trial of flogging, the total number was 198.

Robbery with violence was not, however, the only crime for which flogging was made a penalty after 1861. In 1898 an Act was passed which provided that any male person living on the earnings of prostitution or soliciting for immoral purposes should be deemed a 'rogue and vagabond', within the meaning of the Vagrancy Acts. This meant that the pimp or importuner could henceforth be whipped, but only on a second or subsequent conviction.

During the next few years public feeling grew strongly in favour of improving the existing law so as to deal effectively with the evils of organised prostitution for profit, in particular with the White Slave traffic. The public agitation was to a considerable extent sponsored by the Suffragettes and other feminists of the time, and they promoted a number of Private Members' Bills in Parliament. The passage of these Bills was, however, invariably blocked by M.P.s who were opposed to the extended powers they would give the police of arresting suspected White Slave traffickers without a warrant.

At last the Liberal Government of the day consented to take action. The Home Secretary, Mr. Reginald McKenna, agreed to the infliction of flogging as an addition to the penalties already provided by the Acts dealing with White Slavery and living on immoral earnings. "There are, I am informed," Mr. McKenna told the House of Commons at this time, "a number of young men, almost entirely of foreign origin, who live upon young women to the extent of £10 or £20 a week. They really accumulate fortunes in this way. The police say that the trade is so easy that unless you have some power beyond an ordinary term of imprisonment then you cannot hope to put a stop to it. The police advise that after a conviction has been obtained, if there is a power of flogging, there will be nobody to flog. Flogging can only be administered after a second conviction, and after a first conviction not one of the men will remain in this country any longer."

The result was the passing of a further Criminal Law Amendment Bill in the same year. First, it made the offence of living on the earnings of prostitution and soliciting for immoral purposes floggable after a first conviction, instead of, as previously, after a second conviction. Secondly, it imposed flogging as an additional punishment to the maximum penalty of two years imprisonment with hard labour, for procuring women or girls for immoral purposes, as provided by a previous Criminal Law Amendment Act, passed in 1865.

So far as procuring and living on the immoral earnings of prostitution are concerned (the two offences are combined in the official statistics), there was a sharp rise from fourteen convictions in 1912 to seventy-three in 1913. Thereafter the figures fell rapidly, the annual average of such convictions being seven between 1915 and 1935, which was exactly the same for the years between 1890 and 1910, before the Act. (The majority of these convictions were for living on immoral earnings and not for procuring.) Between 1913 and 1935 only five sentences of corporal punishment were passed for these offences. Also, during the same period only twenty-three sentences were passed out of a total of 974 importuning cases.

One further fact must be added. The League of Nations Commission, which conducted a very careful inquiry into White Slavery between the two world wars, declared itself satisfied that there was no evidence of any traffic in women and children between Great Britain and any foreign country, and that, in their view, it was the Act of 1885 which imposed imprisonment, and not that of 1912 which added flogging, that stamped out this traffic. It is also noteworthy that the figures for rape and defilement of young girls, both non-floggable offences, likewise showed a marked and steady decline during these years.

4

WHIPPING was abolished as a sentence of the court in this country by the Criminal Justice Act 1948, which came into force in September of that year. It applied both to male adult and juvenile delinquents. Since then the lash can be legally inflicted only for serious offences by prisoners against prison discipline on the order of the Prison Visitors. In every such case the punishment has to be approved by the Home Secretary.

What led Parliament to abolish flogging as a judicial punishment? The reason is to be found in the Report of a Departmental Committee on Corporal Punishment which was appointed by the Home Secretary, then Sir John Simon, and the Secretary of State for Scotland, then Mr. Walter Elliot, in 1937. This committee reached the unanimous conclusion that flogging was of no special advantage as a deterrent in respect of those crimes for which it could be inflicted, and that it should be abolished. A majority in both Houses of Parliament agreed with this view.

All the members of this committee were selected as having an open mind on the subject, and none had in any way been previously connected with the movement for the abolition of corporal punishment. Chairman of the committee was Sir Edward Cadogan, a former M.P. and secretary to the Speaker of the House of Commons. There were eight members on the committee besides the chairman. They included an international lawyer, Professor J. L. Brierley; a physician, Sir Robert Hutchison; a retired senior civil servant, Sir William McKechnie; and an ex-judge with considerable experience in the administration of criminal justice, Mr. Cecil Whiteley, K.C., Common Serjeant of London.

The committee held twenty-five meetings and examined seventy-two witnesses orally. These included Recorders, magistrates, prison governors and directors of Borstal Institutions, prison chaplains and medical officers, probation officers, Chief Constables and other police officers. Written evidence was received from the Lord Chief Justice on behalf of the judges of the King's Bench. The Lord Justice General of Scotland was also consulted, but he replied that no flogging sentence had been imposed by any judge of the High Court in Scotland for at least fifty years and in these circumstances the Scottish judges did not feel qualified to express any views on the subject.

The Cadogan Committee began by rejecting the retributive principle—'an eye for an eye and a tooth for a tooth'—as being out of accord with modern theories of penal treatment. Since a sentence of flogging is clearly not reformative, the committee felt that the only other ground on which it could be justified was its value as a deterrent, either in preventing the individual offender from repeating his offence, or in discouraging others. The committee, therefore, made every effort to determine the extent to which a flogging sentence might contain some element of deterrence not provided by a sentence of imprisonment alone.

As to the effect on the individual flogged, there was some division of opinion among the witnesses about whether this form of punishment really deterred him from repeating the offence. Several police witnesses stated that, in their experience, a man who had once been flogged was always careful to avoid committing any further offence for which corporal punishment might be imposed. He might continue to lead a life of crime, but he would avoid crimes for which flogging was a possible penalty. This view was supported by the memorandum submitted by Lord Hewart, the Lord Chief Justice, summarising the views of the judges in England. They considered that flogging operates as a useful deterrent, that it should be retained for existing offences and possibly extended to cover crimes of rape and criminal assaults on young girls.

Some witnesses claimed that no person is ever flogged a second time, but the committee found that this statement was not in accordance with the facts. Though they are not numerous, there have been cases where men who have been flogged have subsequently committed other floggable offences, and in some of these a second flogging sentence has actually been imposed.

Details from the Prison Commissioners' Reports were before the committee. In 1933 a man was flogged twice in the same year, receiving eighteen strokes on the first occasion and twenty-four on the second.

Prison officials and probation officers expressed mixed views. One prison governor recalled two cases in which he had spoken to men who had been flogged for armed robbery. One had said, "Next time I shall take care not to carry a gun." The other had said, "Next time I shall take care to use my gun."

The committee took particular note of the fact that in neither of these two cases had the offender any thought of abandoning robbery altogether.

None of the witnesses suggested that flogging had the effect of restraining the offender from all forms of crime. Even those who believed most strongly in its deterrent value claimed only that it deterred the person punished from committing those special offences for which flogging might be imposed.

After examining all the available evidence the committee members were unable to find any body of facts or figures showing that the introduction of a power of flogging had produced a decrease in the number of crimes for which it could be imposed. While not denying that corporal punishment possesses some deterrent effect, they were not satisfied that it has that exceptionally effective influence as a deterrent which is usually claimed for it by those who advocate its use.

For serious prison offences, such as an attack on a warder, the committee recommended the retention of flogging, but advised the limitation of the maximum number of strokes to eighteen on the medical ground that any further number is likely to cause injury to the tissues out of proportion to any further pain which may be inflicted. (The previous maximum was thirty-six.) The reason why Parliament agreed that a prisoner who assaults a warder can still be flogged is that in his case imprisonment has no longer any deterrent effect, and the only really effective deterrent remaining is the lash.

The Criminal Justice Act has been on the Statute Book for several years. During that period there has been an increase in certain crimes of violence such as felonious wounding, malicious wounding, rape and indecent assault. In 1938, for instance, there were 646 cases of felonious wounding, whereas for 1951 the figure was 1,078. The corresponding figures for indecent assault on females were 3,547 and 4,445 respectively. It should be noted that flogging could not be imposed for any of these offences before 1948.

On the other hand, the late Home Secretary, Sir David Maxwell Fyfe*, pointed out in the House of Commons recently that those crimes of violence which were floggable before 1948 have actually decreased in number since. In 1947 there were 842 armed robberies and robberies with violence in this country. In 1951 the figure was 633. For the first six months of 1952 it was 395.

The question, therefore, which Parliament and the country must consider is not merely whether flogging should be restored for the particular crimes of violence for which it

* Now Lord Kilmuir, Lord Chancellor.

could be imposed before the Criminal Justice Act came into force, but whether the courts should have power to order it for an extended range of offences.

5

CRIMES of violence have increased in the aggregate since the end of the war. In 1945 the numbers were approximately 4,700. In 1951 they had risen to more than 6,500. There is a mounting feeling in the country that the present powers in the hands of the courts are inadequate to deal with the current wave of violent crime, and that the thug who coshes defence-less old men and women and robs them of their savings should be given a dose of his own medicine. Some would go farther and introduce flogging for offences such as blackmail, felonious wounding, rape and other criminal assaults.

Opponents of corporal punishment, on the other hand, believe that to restore flogging now would be a retrograde step. They point out that the crimes, notably armed robbery and robbery with violence, for which flogging could be imposed before its abolition as a judicial sentence by the Criminal Justice Act in 1948 have actually decreased in number since that date.

What view does Parliament take of the question? So far as I can ascertain, opinion is fairly evenly divided. In the Commons, broadly speaking, Tory back-benchers are in favour of restoring flogging, Socialist M.P.s are against it. There are, of course, individual exceptions.

Take Mr. Stanley Evans, Socialist M.P. for Wednesbury, for example. He feels that thugs should not be 'featherbedded' any more than farmers. He favours the return of the birch or 'cat', and so, he adds, do ninety-five per cent of his constituents.

"Why should it be thought right to flog convicts who attack able-bodied warders," asks Mr. Evans, "but wrong to flog work-shy hooligans who attack defenceless old ladies with bicycle chains? I would flog the hides off their backs."

A different view comes from Mr. Christopher Hollis, Conservative M.P. for Devizes. "There has been a decline in offences for which corporal punishment used to be imposed," says Mr. Hollis, "and the nation will make itself ridiculous before the world if it reintroduces it."

The Government have hitherto refrained from expressing any view one way or the other. But the Chancellor, Lord Kilmuir, is known to be against any proposal to reintroduce corporal punishment at the moment. His views, guided as they must be to some extent by the expert advice available in his late department, will no doubt carry considerable weight with the Prime Minister and the Cabinet. What Sir David feels is that the Criminal Justice Act should be given a longer trial before this Parliament reverses the work of its predecessor.

It is difficult to assess the feeling in the House of Lords as a whole. If the peers were to turn up in strength, the majority would probably vote to restore flogging. Lord Goddard, the Lord Chief Justice, and other law lords, in particular, favour bringing it back.

When the Criminal Justice Bill was before the Upper House in 1948, Lord Goddard moved an amendment which was designed to give the courts power to order the birch but not the 'cat'. He did so, he has said, not because he thought the 'cat' was a terrible instrument—it is in fact no longer a terrible instrument—but because a man who has been given the 'cat' is too often looked upon by his fellows as a hero.

The birch, on the other hand, gives a certain amount of pain while certainly leaving no marks, and it often led to considerable ridicule when the offender came out. "And nothing kills quicker than ridicule," added the Lord Chief Justice.

Lord Goddard's amendment was accepted by the House of Lords but was subsequently deleted by the Commons when they came to reconsider the Bill. The peers, consequently, did not insist upon it.

I should not be surprised if history were to repeat itself. Just as M.P.s made garrotting a floggable offence ninety years ago against the advice of the Home Secretary of the day, the Commons may well decide, regardless of Ministerial views, that so far as concerns flogging the Criminal Justice Act has now had a fair trial and that the courts should be given back the powers which that Act took away from them in 1948.

It will certainly be argued that as the convict is today largely restrained from attacking prison warders by the knowledge that he will almost certainly get the 'cat' if he does so, the thug outside will likewise be influenced by the fear of the lash.

I have no doubt, too, that the views of Lord Goddard and other Queen's Bench judges will be quoted to the effect that before 1948 no accused man would ever plead guilty to robbery with violence. They would often offer to plead guilty to robbery, but never robbery with violence—because they were afraid of the painful consequences to their skins which would inevitably follow such a plea.

On the other hand, it will be argued that at the present time the only countries in the world to retain flogging in their penal code are certain parts of the British Commonwealth and, to a very limited extent, the United States of America and ourselves. It will be argued, too, that to restore flogging is to put the clock back, particularly as pre-1948 floggable offences have shown a steady decline.

Ultimately the question whether to flog or not is one that cannot be resolved on any basis other than individual opinion.

VI. THE PROBLEM OF THE YOUNG OFFENDER

VI. THE PROBLEM OF THE YOUNG OFFENDER

1. Changes in the Law

WITHOUT doubt one of the most urgent problems of the present time is that of the young criminal or, in the language of Whitehall, the juvenile delinquent. Of course, it is no new problem. Two hundred and fifty years ago Pope Clement XI addressed himself to it when he built in Rome the world's first reformatory 'for the correction and instruction of wayward boys'.

In Britain today the problem remains as acute as formerly, in spite of the modern paraphernalia of juvenile courts, approved schools, attendance and detention centres, child psychologists, probation and after-care. Indeed the amount of youthful crime has doubled since before the last war. In 1951, for instance, approximately 28,500 young people under fourteen were found guilty by Magistrates' Courts compared with 15,500 in 1938. The figures of convictions in the higher courts for the same period were, for those under seventeen, 600 in 1951, compared with 240 in 1938, and for those between seventeen and twenty-one, 4,000 in 1951, compared with 2,000 in 1938.

Commenting on this increase in a debate in the House of Lords in 1948, Lord Jowitt, who was Lord Chancellor at the time, said, "We do not want to exaggerate these figures, and, of course, it is the fact that the great majority of the people of this country lead decent, honest law-abiding lives. But the truth is that a trend like this is a matter which must cause grave concern to every right-thinking man and woman."

The increase has been particularly marked among the youths who have grown up under Britain's Welfare State. It has culminated in the shocking cases of Christopher Craig and Derek Bentley, recently convicted of murdering a police constable who was trying to arrest them for breaking into a warehouse.

It is a sad reflection on our times that both these youths were found at their trial to be practically illiterate. At the age of nineteen Bentley could scarcely sign his name, and the letter which he sent his parents on the eve of his execution had to be dictated and taken down by a warder in the condemned cell.

The gangster film and the comic strip are by no means wholly to blame for this shocking state of affairs, although no doubt they form a contributory factor in setting the erring child and youth on the downward path. The fundamental cause of juvenile delinquency must be sought in conditions of environment in the home: both physical and moral, such as overcrowding and the lack of unity and happiness in family life.

But what of the remedies? Today the penalties which the courts can award to the youthful offender are limited to probation, fines, Borstal training and sending to an approved school, attendance or detention centre. No one under seventeen can now be imprisoned and, since 1948, no sentences of corporal punishment can be imposed.

Are these remedies sufficient deterrents? Have we not possibly gone too far in the direction of leniency in dealing with the young criminal? Should not the sterner methods of former times be tried? Or at least is there not a case for the treatment described by Lord Chief Justice Goddard as 'a good larruping', and which that eminent judge has on more than one occasion publicly regretted that he had not the power to order?

No one, I think, would wish to return to the evil practice, which continued into the present century, whereby boys and girls were not merely tried by the same courts as adult criminals but were punished by imprisonment in the same gaols.

Visitors to the Tate Gallery will remember Lady Stanley's moving picture entitled 'His First Offence'. It shows a ragged little urchin standing behind the rails of the dock, his small face expressing an agony of fear. Such a scene could not be repeated in our courts today, and few amongst us would probably wish it to. Specially constituted courts for dealing with juvenile offenders have been operating successfully in this country for the past forty-five years and no sane person would like to see them abolished.

Similarly, we would not wish to send youngsters to prison along with hardened adult criminals. The harmfulness of the old system was pointed out as long ago as 1880 by the then Home Secretary, Sir William Harcourt, in a letter to Queen Victoria. "The child who has been guilty only of some mischievous or thoughtless prank which does not partake of the real character of crime finds himself committed with adult criminals guilty of heinous offences to the common jail," wrote Harcourt. "After a week or a fortnight's imprisonment he comes out of prison tainted in character amongst his former companions . . . and he soon lapses into the criminal class with whom he has been identified."

It may be added here that at the time Harcourt wrote there were already some reformatory schools in existence. Forerunners of approved schools and Borstal, these institutions came into being and were made subject to inspection largely as the result of the case of a boy of fifteen who committed suicide in prison in the 1850s. But the training which they provided was extremely limited, for boys the emphasis being on agricultural work and for girls on preparation for domestic service.

The actual plight of the youngster in prison in the old days was vividly described by Oscar Wilde in a letter which he wrote to the *Daily Chronicle* when he came out of prison in 1897, protesting against the dismissal of a warder in Reading prison for having given some biscuits to a hungry child.

The cruelty that is practised by day and night on children in English prisons is incredible, except to those who have witnessed it and are aware of the brutality of the system . . . the present treatment of children is terrible, primarily from people not understanding the peculiar psychology of a child's nature. A child can understand a punishment inflicted by an individual, such as a parent or guardian, and can bear it with a certain amount of acquiescence. What it cannot understand is a punishment inflicted by society. It cannot realise what society is . . . the child consequently, being taken away from its parents by people whom it has never seen, and of whom it knows nothing, and finding itself in a lonely and unfamiliar cell, waited on by strange faces, and ordered about and punished by the representatives of a system it cannot understand, becomes an immediate prey to the first and most prominent emotion produced by modern prison life—the emotion of terror. . . .

Of course no child under fourteen years of age should be sent to prison at all. It is an absurdity, and, like many absurdities, of absolutely tragic results. . . .

Wilde's plaintive words did not pass unheeded, although children continued for some years longer to be sent to prison for quite trifling offences. In 1899, for instance, a boy of eleven was sentenced to imprisonment with hard labour in one of Her Majesty's gaols for damaging a door.

The change came with the return of a Liberal Government to power in the early years of the present century. The Probation of Offenders Act of 1907 for the first time provided a means of reinforcing parental control in the child's own home through the agency of trained social workers. This was immediately followed by an equally important legislative measure, the Children Act of 1908, which abolished the imprisonment of children and instituted juvenile courts. It is perhaps worth noting that in respect both of probation and juvenile courts we were anticipated by the United States, where the first probation law was introduced, in Massachusetts, in 1878, and the first juvenile court, in Illinois, in 1899.

In 1933 came the Children and Young Persons Act, which governs the work of the modern juvenile court in this country. This Act insists that in every case the court shall consider the child's welfare. At the same time the Rules made by the Lord Chancellor under its provisions expressly provide that every juvenile court shall be composed of justices 'specially qualified' to deal with the cases that come before it. This Act was described as the 'Children's Charter' when it was before Parliament, since its underlying purpose in its application to young offenders is reformation rather than punishment.

Finally, in 1948, the Criminal Justice Act made a further important contribution to the treatment of juvenile crime. It provided the courts with two new remedies and at the same time took away a time-honoured old one.

The two new remedies are the attendance centre and the detention centre, to which youngsters between twelve and twenty-one can be sent for offences for which, if they were adults, they might be sent to prison.

The remedy which the Act abolished was the birch, although this had largely ceased to be ordered by most juvenile courts for many years.

In the following pages we shall look at the composition and working of the juvenile courts, the effectiveness of the corrective treatment at their disposal, and the general domestic background of the young offender.

2. JUVENILE COURTS

LET us take a look at the juvenile courts, of which there are nearly a thousand in England and Wales, since these are the institutions charged with the treatment of the young offender in the first instance. How are they constituted? And what sort of a job are they doing today?

The English juvenile court is a court of summary jurisdiction, its constitution being governed by the Children and Young Person's Act 1933, and by Rules made by the Lord Chancellor under its provisions. The Act requires that "every court in dealing with a child or young person, who is brought before it, either as being in need of care or protection or as an offender or otherwise, *shall have regard to the welfare of the child or young person* and shall in a proper case take steps for removing him from undesirable surroundings and for securing that proper provision is made for his education and training." (My italics.)

The court consists of a chairman and two other magistrates, preferable one of either sex, although in an emergency the chairman is empowered to sit with one other magistrate only. These justices, according to the Lord Chancellor's Rules, must be "specially qualified for dealing with juvenile cases". They are chosen from a panel which is reconstituted every three years.

In London the chairman and other members of the panel are appointed by the Home Secretary. Elsewhere the chairman is elected by his colleagues on the panel, who in turn are chosen by the vote of the whole body of justices for the petty sessional division concerned.

Incidentally, a 'child' becomes in law a 'young person' at the age of fourteen and as such is subject to certain variations of procedure, both as regards trial and treatment. With two exceptions 'children' must be tried summarily for all offences, whereas in the case of indictable offences 'young persons' may, if they wish, go for trial before a jury at quarter sessions or assizes—in practice they usually elect to be tried summarily. The exceptions are murder and manslaughter, the only offences which, by reason of their grave character, may not be tried by juvenile courts. Thus the scope of these courts as criminal courts is far wider than any other court of summary juris-diction and, it need hardly be added, the responsibility cast upon the Bench of magistrates is considerably heavier. Offenders over the age of seventeen must, in general, be tried by the ordinary courts.

The officials of the juvenile court include the clerk, the probation officers and, in the larger courts, an usher. The probation officers are experienced social workers of both sexes, not civil servants like the clerk of the court, but responsible to the court and paid jointly by the local authority and the central government. Since 1925 there must be at least one probation officer in every petty sessional division or combined group of divisions.

Members of the general public are not admitted to the court except by special permission of the Bench. The Press, on the other hand, are allowed to attend and to report the proceedings, although they may no longer publish the name, address or school, or include any particulars calculated to lead to the identification of any defendant concerned.

The Act of 1933 also provides that juvenile courts shall sit either in a different building or room from that in which other courts are held, or else on different days from the other courts. In the larger cities, at least, the courts sit in some building which has nothing to do with the ordinary police court and which is not associated in the minds of the public with crime and criminals.

So far as the court room itself is concerned, simplicity is the key note. There are none of the traditional features of the ordinary criminal court, no raised bench, no railed dock, no benches for counsel—not even the Royal Coat of Arms on the wall behind the chairman. The main equipment consists of tables and chairs and a simple witness-box. The delinquents charged stand behind a chalk line facing the magistrate's table, while their parents are seated immediately behind them. The parents' presence is compulsory, unless the court decides that there are particular reasons for excusing them from attendance.

Some people have criticised the informality of this court, on the ground that the majesty of the law ought to be retained so as to impress the older wrongdoers. But it is probably true to say that little would be gained by approximating the scene more closely to the ordinary court. The older boys and girls would no doubt acquire a sense of self-importance which it is desirable to avoid at all costs, while the younger ones would merely be frightened, which is equally undesirable, since many of them have probably been frightened already.

I believe that the magistrates who sit in the juvenile courts of this country are on the whole doing excellent work, often in trying circumstances which call for the exercise of an abundance of patience, understanding, kindness and common sense. As the Royal Commission put it, in reviewing the existing arrangements in 1946, the need is for men and women who have not merely a love of children, but a real appreciation of the surroundings and way of life of the type of child who most frequently finds his way into the juvenile court. Many of them possess a rich store of experience, like Mr. Basil Henriques, Chairman of the East London Juvenile Court, and Mr. John Watson, Chairman of the South-East London Court.

Hitherto the principal drawback has been the preponderance of elderly juvenile justices and to a lesser extent the absence of women from the panels. The former has to some extent been corrected by the Lord Chancellor's Rules made in 1950 that no justice who is not a stipendiary magistrate may be a member of a panel after reaching the age of sixty-five. At that date sixty per cent of the juvenile court justices were between fifty and seventy. The position has improved somewhat since then, but there are still too many elderly justices of grandparental age sitting on the juvenile court benches. Also there are still some panels, about a dozen in all, which have no women members.

Just as the surroundings of the juvenile court should be simple, so the proceedings should be conducted in language which can be understood by the children and young persons appearing before it. This is not always the case, magistrates and others sometimes employing the technical phraseology of the adult courts, to the bewilderment of the young defendants. Mr. John Watson tells a story of a small boy brought before one of the Metropolitan courts during the war. A police witness used the word 'recognisance' in giving his evidence, and the chairman intervened to explain what it meant. To his surprise the boy said he knew perfectly well. "Course I knows what it is," he declared. "It's what our airplanes does over Germany every night."

The delinquents who toe the chalk line in the juvenile courts appear on a variety of charges. Most common of the indictable offences are larcenies of various kinds. These are, in the main, of toys, sweets, cigarettes, or money to buy them with, or of easily negotiable property. Next come shop-breaking, receiving property knowing it to have been stolen, sexual offences and other assaults. There are also cases of frauds and false pretences and also robbery. Recently, for instance, a small boy broke into a shop and stole £500 in cash, nearly all of which he contrived to spend or give away before he was caught. Of the non-indictable offences cycling offences are the most common. Next comes malicious damage. And, it may be added, offences under this latter heading are not always of a minor character. Quite recently a London court had to deal with two children, aged eight, who broke into a pharmaceutical store and, in an orgy of wanton destruction, did damage amounting to £1,300.

Juvenile prostitution is by no means uncommon. Many of the girls on the streets of our larger cities are precociously developed and on physical examination are found to be fully-grown young women. One girl, seen some years ago, though only sixteen, was found to have already banked £1,600.

When a boy or girl has been found guilty, the court has various courses open to it, some of them depending on the age of the offender. He or she may be discharged, either absolutely or conditionally, released on probation, fined, ordered to attend at an attendance centre, committed to a remand home, sent to an approved school or a Borstal institution, or—and this is the latest treatment—confined in a detention centre. In addition the parent or guardian may be ordered to pay the fine on the delinquent's behalf and may also be directed to enter into a recognisance by giving security for the good behaviour of the child. Always, however, the paramount consideration of the court is, or should be, the child's welfare, as indeed is required by the statute.

3. CORRECTIVE TREATMENT

WE must now consider the various forms of treatment of young offenders open to juvenile courts. Broadly speaking they fall into two main categories, treatment at home and treatment away from home.

Some courts are still inclined to treat juvenile delinquents like defaulting motorists, imposing a 5s. fine for the first offence, 10s. for the second, and so on, without always making inquiries as they should into the offender's background, which is an indispensable preliminary to corrective treatment.

Take the comparatively recent case of a boy of fourteen, convicted of stealing margarine from a shop. He had been guilty of one previous offence of breaking and entering. The facts disclosed that his mother was in bad health, suffering from cataract in both eyes. She had nine children by a previous marriage, eleven by this one. The father was a heavy drinker who used foul language at home. He had seduced one of the stepdaughters during the wife's absence in hospital. In this case the magistrates might have sent the boy to an approved school so as to remove him from an obviously harmful environment, or at least they might have put him under the care of the probation officer. Instead they fined him half a crown!

In every case where a child or young person has been found guilty the probation officer should first investigate and report on his or her home surroundings, school record, health and character. Sometimes the Bench also calls for a psychologist's report and will recommend a course of psychiatric treatment. This is frequently prescribed in sexual cases. Sometimes, too, the Bench will enlist the parents' advice in court. "What do you think we ought to do about Harry?" "He's got to be learnt a lesson," one mother will answer; "he can't go on like this." Others, perhaps the majority, will say, "He's a good boy, really. He won't do it again. Don't send him away, sir."

Now, as to the treatment the court may order. I use the word 'treatment' rather than 'punishment', since punishment, though often necessary is only one of the forms of correction open to the court.

First of all there is discharge, which may be either absolute or conditional. The former is not an acquittal, but is tantamount to being let off with a caution. Needless to say, it should never be ordered unless investigation has revealed a family background beyond reproach and the court is satisfied that the offence is an isolated incident which is unlikely to be repeated. In a conditional discharge, on the other hand, the offender is set free on the understanding that, if he gets into trouble again during the period of the order, he may be brought back and dealt with for the original offence as well as for the new one. It is sometimes ordered where the court feels that supervision by a probation officer is unnecessary.

In most cases, however, where the circumstances are too serious to warrant absolute discharge and the court decides to give the offender a chance to prove himself, he is put on probation. This means that he is placed under the supervision of one of the local probation officers, a trained social worker, for a period of not less than one nor more than three years. The court may impose various requirements when making the probation order, such as that, should the probationer live in an approved probation hostel or with relatives; until the order expires, he suffers no punishment. If he fails to do so or gets into further trouble, he may be punished for the original offence, as in the case of a conditional discharge.

The weakness of the present probation system is that there are not enough probation officers of the right type. Some of them have sixty cases or more to look after and they obviously cannot give all the children the individual attention they require, particularly in the early stages of the probationary period. Another drawback is that probation does not act as a deterrent on the delinquent's companions, who in many cases are inclined to think that he 'has got away with it'. Nevertheless there is reason to believe that something like seventy per cent of probationers 'go straight' afterwards.

A new experiment in treatment at home is the attendance centre, which has come into being as the result of the Criminal Justice Act 1948. Offenders between the ages of twelve and twenty-one may be ordered by the court to attend at these centres for periods not exceeding twelve hours in all and not more than three hours in any one day, the times of attendance being arranged so as not to interfere with education or employment. This may not seem much, but discipline is strict—no talking and no smoking are allowed—and when spread over six successive Saturdays attendance may be regarded as having a strong deterrent effect. The curriculum includes physical training and instruction in such subjects as handicrafts, first aid and citizenship. Briefly, the aim is to encourage the boys and girls to make proper use of their leisure time, and it is hoped that the activities of the centres will encourage the attendants to join local youth organisations. Only a few of these centres have been opened so far, eight in all, and it is too soon yet to say whether they will justify an extension of the scheme.

In the field of treatment away from home there are the approved schools, Borstal institutions, for older offenders, and another experiment under the Criminal Justice Act, the detention centre.

Approved schools, or, as they are sometimes called, Home Office Schools, of which there are ninety-three for boys and forty-three for girls in England and Wales, differ from other schools in that the children are removed from the care of their parents and compelled to reside in the school and undergo the training provided. They are mostly administered by voluntary bodies, but some come directly under the local authority. None of them, however, may operate except subject to Home Office approval and inspection. Except for the limitation of residence and twenty-four holidays a year, they are virtually indistinguishable from ordinary boarding schools. It costs an average of six guineas a week to keep a boy or girl at an approved school. Children or young persons may be sent there if they are guilty of an offence which in the case of an adult would be punishable by imprisonment, and also for a number of other reasons such as being 'beyond control', non-attendance at school, and if they are found by the court to be 'in need of care or protection'.

Approved schools can by no means be regarded as an unqualified success. Subsequent case histories show that thirty-four per cent of boys and sixteen per cent of girls get into trouble again after leaving. About eleven per cent of approved school boys subsequently go to Borstal or prison.

Nor has the administration of these schools left nothing to be desired. In 1947 public opinion was gravely disturbed to learn that a member of the staff of an approved school in Staffordshire had been shot dead by one of a party of boys who, largely because their release on licence had been deferred, had resolved to abscond and had stolen service rifles from the school armoury and ammunition from the headmaster's house. From the boys' own account it had been their intention to murder the headmaster, but the appearance on the scene of a junior member of the staff led to his becoming the victim instead. This shocking crime led to a much needed overhaul in administration of these schools, particularly as regards the licensing of the boys.

Borstal, which exists for the benefit of older offenders, boys and girls between seventeen and twenty-one, is not a penal institution in the accepted sense of the word. The system, which takes its name from the village in Kent where the first experiments of its kind were made more than forty years ago, exists to provide training, in the words of its Statutory Rules, so as "to bring to bear every influence which may establish in the inmates the will to lead a good and useful life on release, and to fit them to do so by the fullest possible development of their character, capacities, and sense of personal responsibility". Thus although discipline is stricter than in the approved school and there is greater emphasis placed on hard work, the aim is essentially the same.

About half the youth released from Borstal are reconvicted, but many of those manage to 'go straight' after a second period of training. In general three out of every ten boys and two out of every ten girls revert to a life of crime. At present there are about 3,000 boys and 300 girls undergoing training in Borstal institutions.

So far only one detention centre has been opened. It is situated at Kidlington in Oxfordshire and is designed to provide a 'short sharp shock' for boys between fourteen and seventeen who are unlikely to respond to probation, but for whom the prolonged residential training of an approved school is inappropriate. The normal period of detention is two and a half months. The prime features are brisk activity under strict discipline and supervision, with no entertainments. Here is the time-table of an average day.

6.15 a.m.	Rise, wash—air beds.
6.35	P.T. and morning run
6.50	Make beds—dress for work
7.15	Breakfast
8–12 noon	Work
12 noon	Dinner
1–4.30 p.m.	Work or school and P.T.
4.30	Wash and change
5	Tea
6–8.30	Domestic chores, silent study, further education, gym and recreation
8.30	Supper
9	Bed
9.30	Lights out

Since the detention centre was only opened in August, 1952, and relatively few boys have so far been sent there, it is too soon to form a considered estimate of its value. But there is already evidence of its deterrent effect. One boy has stated that he "hated every minute of it" and another has testified that anyone who asked for a second dose "must be mad".

In all these forms of corrective treatment the court has stepped into the parents' shoes. But neither the guidance of the most experienced probation officer nor the discipline of the detention centre or the best of approved schools can compensate for the lack of a good home and wise parental control.

4.   PUNISHMENT AND THE HOME BACKGROUND

PUNISHMENT, as we have seen, is only one of the methods of treating juvenile crime. From time to time it is necessary for the courts to award a sharp penalty which will act as a deterrent. With members of the older school, who have memories of punishments they underwent at school or at home with no apparent ill effects, this usually meant one thing—the stick. They condemn as sloppy sentimentality the spirit which moved Parliament in 1948 to abolish whipping as a judicial sentence, alike for juveniles and adults.

These arm-chair critics are apt to overlook two important factors. First, their own childhood surroundings were vastly different from the home conditions of the average child or 'young person' who finds his way into a juvenile court today. Secondly, corporal punishment as administered by a boy's parent or schoolmaster is very different from that ordered by a Bench of magistrates. It is one thing for a boy coming from a good home to be beaten by his father whom he loves, or by a master whom he at least respects, immediately after he has committed the offence for which he is being punished. It is quite another thing for a boy, often coming from a poor and overcrowded home, to be birched by a police officer whom he has never seen before, after a considerable time has elapsed.

Personally I see no objection to occasional beatings in the

home or school, provided that if the boy fails to respond to this treatment something else should be tried. The relationship between him and his parent or master is a continuing one, and he bears the latter no lasting ill-will afterwards. Judicial birchings, on the other hand, are, or rather were, liable to make a hero out of the mischievous boy and, in the case of the nervously unstable or mentally unbalanced boy, to do more harm than good. That is why the more enlightened juvenile courts many years ago ceased to order this form of punishment, why successive Home Office Departmental Committees recommended its abolition, and why Parliament by the Criminal Justice Act of 1948 rightly decided to put this recommendation into effect.

During the First World War, when juvenile crime was on the increase as it is today, Sir William Clarke Hall, the pioneer of juvenile court work in London and an acknowledged authority on the treatment of young offenders, kept a record of cases heard at the Shoreditch courts over which he presided. He found that of all the children charged with a subsequent offence thirty-five per cent had originally been birched, a larger proportion than in the case of any other form of treatment. He consequently decided to abandon the use of the birch, because he was satisfied that it was not an effective deterrent, and his example was followed with equally encouraging results by other juvenile courts. In 1920 over 1,300 juveniles were birched. By 1939 this figure had fallen to 58, and, although it rose sharply during the Second World War to nearly 500, it rapidly decreased as the inefficiency of this punishment again became apparent, and by 1947 there were only eight cases of judicial birching of juveniles.

The conduct of the delinquent juvenile is often directly attributable to that of the delinquent parent. It is usually when the parents have failed in their duty to the child that the trouble begins. Many cases are due to the wilful neglect or selfishness of the father or mother. Probation officers have found undernourished children in a filthy home, which at the same time boasts a television set that is being paid for by one of the parents on the instalment system. The courts subsequently try to stand in the parents' shoes, but with all the remedies at their disposal they can never hope completely to replace the loving care of a good father and mother. In the case of a neglectful parent who has been indifferent to the child's welfare, the court will sometimes bind him over to give security for the child's future good behaviour in a considerable amount, such as £25 or even £50, since the parent might be tempted to disregard the possible forfeiture of a smaller sum and persist in his neglect. By explaining to the juvenile that if he gets into further trouble his father will have to pay up on his account, the chairman of the Bench also tries to instil a sense of responsibility into the child.

To make a good citizen the child must learn to control his desires and actions so that they may harmonise with the good of the community. In other words, he must be civilised. As a baby he is completely uncivilised; in this state his natural impulse is to take what he wants. As he grows up he must be brought to realise that he must not take what is harmful to him or what does not belong to him. His behaviour is influenced in the first place by the environment of his home. Most children find their way into the courts because they have not learnt to control themselves or recognise the rights of others. The juvenile court cannot itself administer the necessary corrective treatment. All it can do is to decide on the course of treatment which it considers best for the child's welfare and rely on a selected agency to carry it out.

Sometimes low mentality makes it difficult for a child to understand the complex conditions of modern life or to foresee the result of his actions. There is the case of one boy who was charged on a number of occasions with stealing bicycle wheels. He owned a bicycle himself, and his method was to remove the wheel from someone else's machine, leaving one of his own in its place. It turned out that he had not grasped the fact that punctures could be mended. When he got a puncture, he simply went and looked for another wheel with an unpunctured tyre. Treatment of cases like this where the child has not developed any positive anti-social attitude is relatively easy to deal with. It is much more difficult when he has developed a rooted opposition to civilising influences. Thus he may be in a state of emotional upset through parental misunderstanding or maltreatment, and this may lead him to reject the influences first of the family and then of society. One of the most frequent forms of misbehaviour in such circumstances is stealing, although the connection between the offence and the emotional stress from which the child is suffering is not always clear to the magistrates. Here it is possible for psychiatry to render a useful service in tracing and ultimately curing the cause of the emotional disturbance.

To say that some offenders are bad and others ill is not, of course, to palliate the offences. Firm training over a long period may be required to make the delinquent respond to civilising influences. Punishment, as we have seen, plays its part, but the part which it plays is, or should be, only relative. No sane person would deny the need for punishing a naughty child when he or she deserves it. If this is done in a good home by a loving parent, the child understands it. It is much more difficult for the child to understand it when the punishment is inflicted by society. That is why the emphasis in the juvenile courts has shifted largely from the punitive to the reformative. Some people consider that the shift has been too great and that the juvenile delinquents should have more 'good larrupings' as recently recommended by the Lord Chief Justice. However that may be, the juvenile courts are still confronted with the difficult task of diagnosing which cases are likely to respond to the choice of forms of treatment open to them.

5. WHAT IS THE BEST CURE?

WE have now surveyed the increase in juvenile crime and noted its principal causes, we have looked at the work of the juvenile courts and we have examined the various forms of treatment open to them in dealing with the youthful criminal. It remains to consider whether the complex and costly modern apparatus for the treatment of juvenile delinquency is justified by results. In other words, should we continue with the present system, which is designed to reform rather than punish? Or should we conclude in the light of events that it has failed in its purpose and return to the sterner methods of our fathers? If we are to carry on, is the present system capable of improvement?

It is an immense problem, and one on which there is no dearth of information and opinion. There are dozens of books on juvenile delinquency, masses of figures and case histories capable of analysis, scores of theories on the subject of treatment. Several 'documentaries' have been made for the screen, and a feature film, *Cosh Boy*, has recently been shown in London. A recent play, *Now Barabbas*, which was also filmed, takes young offenders inside prison as its central characters.

Here is the view of the author of *Now Barabbas*, Mr. W. Douglas Home, who served a sentence for a military offence in war-time (refusing to attack a civilian-occupied French town). "I studied some two or three thousand prisoners during my stay in two English jails," Mr. Home has stated, "and I arrived at the conclusion that no more than ten per cent were 'criminals', by which I mean, to use the Bible's phraseology, 'men possessed of devils' that could never be cast out . . . I contend that, for the remaining ninety per cent, medical aid and not a punitive approach is far more likely to effect a cure."

This is a far-reaching point of view, and one which will not find favour with many people who prefer to regard individuals as in the main responsible for their actions and who consequently distrust any tendency to treat crime as a form of disease. They deplore what they consider to be excessive pampering of naughty children. "When I did wrong," they will say, "I was not sent to a psychiatrist, but bent over and caned." This view is reflected on the Bench, among magistrates and judges. The predilection of the Lord Chief Justice for naughty boys to have 'a good larruping' is well known. Another High Court judge expressed himself in even stronger language a few years ago when he learned in a case before him that a father had broken a stick over his son's back. "There should be more breaking of sticks over boys' backs," remarked this judge. "Perhaps they would then behave better."

My own view, I would say, lies somewhere between these two extremes, probably nearer Mr. Home's than Lord Goddard's. There is no magic about psychiatric treatment. Nor is it fair to regard psychologists and psychiatrists as cranks. On the contrary, they are usually fully-qualified doctors who specialise in complaints of the mind, just as physicians and surgeons specialise in those of the body. The present tendency is for magistrates, particularly those in juvenile courts, more and more frequently to remand the delinquent for a psychologist's report. This has the effect of bringing out more clearly the causes of the delinquent acts and also of illuminating the degree and inner nature of the mind disturbance in the individual case. It can be of particular value where the court is considering some drastic step, such as taking the child away from home, or is doubtful about the treatment it should order and desires confirmation of statements made by the child or its parents. Important, however, as is psychiatry in the sphere of investigation, where it should be encouraged and extended, there is still need for improved facilities for psychiatric treatment. Here a beginning has been made within the approved school system, where in a few of the schools a psychiatrist attends weekly to give treatment in suitable cases. There is much to be said for extending these arrangements.

Another urgent need is for more probation officers. These trained social workers are by and large doing an excellent job, but, I venture to think, there are far too few of them. One such officer may have as many as sixty cases 'on his books', and, with the best will in the world and the most lavish expenditure of shoe leather, it is difficult for this overworked individual to keep in full and complete touch with every case and give it the amount of attention it may need.

The magistrates' Benches are also in need of reinforcement and indeed of further overhaul. There are still too many elderly magistrates, who have been included in their local commissions of the peace as a reward for political services. There are still magistrates, too, sitting on judicial courts who have never taken a course of instruction, who have never studied such great legislative enactments as the Children and Young

Persons Act of 1933 and the Criminal Justice Act of 1948, who have never read a book on juvenile delinquency and who habitually ignore the Home Office circulars issued for their guidance.

The reactionary views of many justices are exemplified in the recent ballot conducted by the Magistrates Association where 4,500 magistrates voted for the return of corporal punishment, a majority of two to one. By contrast, it should be noted, the probation officers voted six to one against having back the birch and even the minority in favour of its reintroduction thought that there should be some safeguards and that the punishment should only be imposed by order of the higher courts.

The House of Commons has also rejected by a decisive majority (159 votes to 63) a Private Member's Bill designed to restore whipping for crimes of violence. The result was due, in part at least, to the statesmanlike intervention of the late Home Secretary, Sir David Maxwell Fyfe, who argued that it would be premature to reverse the provisions of the 1948 Act about flogging until there had been more time to assess the effects of the whole scheme of corrective training and preventive detention which that measure had introduced. He hoped, he said, soon to open more detention centres and attendance centres for young offenders in spite of the difficulties of the capital investment programme, and to get more camps and castles and anything else capable of improving the accommodation of delinquents.

In the same debate the then Home Secretary made it clear that the Government was not in any sense complacent about the current crime wave. Proof of this may be seen in the Prevention of Crime Act, which became law in 1953. This measure, which empowers a police officer to arrest anyone he suspects of committing a crime, or being about to commit a crime, with an offensive weapon, throws the onus upon the possessor of the weapon of proving that it is not being used for an illegal purpose. Persons convicted of carrying such weapons 'without lawful authority or excuse' are liable to a fine or imprisonment. This measure should certainly act as a more effective deterrent to the 'cosh boy', and also as a greater protection to the community, than giving the courts once more the power to flog.

There has also got to be an increase in our police force, both of men and women, because that obviously affects the sphere of crime prevention. They should have fewer hours on duty and more attractive rates of pay. The Government is trying to increase recruitment to this force, according to the late Home Secretary, but although the figures are improving in some parts of the country, there is still an appreciable lag in the larger cities, notably London, Manchester, Liverpool, Birmingham and Bristol.

Finally, we must all do whatever we can, in Sir David Maxwell Fyfe's words, "to improve the weakening moral standards of our time". Much crime can undoubtedly be traced to the lowering of general standards of conduct as regards controls, not regarded as morally binding, and property generally, private or public.

This brings us back to the core of the problem of the young offender—the home. No amount of corrective treatment imposed from without, whether by juvenile courts, approved schools, or detention centres, can compensate any child or youth for the lack of a good home life. So long as there are morally delinquent parents there will be criminally delinquent children. The best the law can do is to try to correct the evil by the most scientific methods, but it is only a second best. Delinquency, like charity, begins at home, and home is where it can best be cured.